HOW TO
BEAT
TRUMP

ALSO BY MARK HALPERIN

Double Down: Game Change 2012
with John Heilemann

*Game Change: Obama and the Clintons, McCain
and Palin, and the Race of a Lifetime*
with John Heilemann

The Undecided Voter's Guide to the Next President

The Way to Win: Taking the White House in 2008
with John F. Harris

HOW TO BEAT TRUMP

AMERICA'S TOP POLITICAL STRATEGISTS ON
WHAT IT WILL TAKE

MARK HALPERIN

Regan
Arts.

Regan Arts.

Copyright © Mark Halperin, 2019

First Regan Arts paperback edition, November 2019

Library of Congress Control Number: 2019948790

ISBN 978-1-68245-127-4

Interior design by Aubrey Khan, Neuwirth & Associates
Cover image by Xinhua / Alamy Stock Photo

Printed in the United States of America

For my father.

TABLE OF CONTENTS

"NOTHING IS SO PAINFUL
TO THE HUMAN MIND AS A
GREAT AND SUDDEN CHANGE."
—MARY WOLLSTONECRAFT SHELLEY, *FRANKENSTEIN*

TRUMP CAN WIN AGAIN

Long ago, way back in the fall of 2003, tens of millions of Americans knew three things were true about President George W. Bush:

He would lose reelection to the Democratic nominee in November 2004.

The future of the country depended on his defeat.

There would never be a worse president of the United States.

As the nation began gearing up for the 2004 presidential cycle, President Bush was looking at a tough reelection battle. His approval ratings had plummeted, and the political and personal boost he had received in the wake of the September 11, 2001, terrorist attacks had given way to a progression of bad news both at home and abroad.

Bush's economic record was abysmal. Almost three million American jobs had been lost during his tenure, family incomes had declined sharply, the number of citizens without health insurance had risen substantially, and poverty was rampant.

His foreign policy record was now defined by the human and financial costs of the war in Iraq, an unwinnable conflict Bush had begun based on a false claim that Saddam Hussein had weapons of mass destruction.

There was no peace. There was no prosperity. Republicans were distressed, despairing; Democrats were breezily confident. Bush, it was said, was doomed. James Carville, one of the keenest campaign strategists of the modern era, declared at the time that if Bush were victorious over the Democratic nominee "it would be the greatest political achievement of my lifetime."

Bush won reelection, beating Senator John Kerry of Massachusetts by a slim but definitive margin. His second term was notable for sputtering domestic policies, the natural and managerial disasters of Hurricane Katrina, and the 2008 financial crisis. Although Bush departed the White House with tens of millions abhorring him, his eight years in office are now regarded with nostalgia, if not quite appreciation. He is no longer considered by those tens of millions to be the worst president in American history.

That honor is held by Donald J. Trump.

And now, with the 2020 election upon us, we are looking at a parallel dynamic from sixteen years ago, amplified by the gargantuan and garish persona of Trump, loved and loathed with unprecedented intensity. Those who admire him will cheerfully don their MAGA hats; seek out his bacchanalian rallies; ignore his misdeeds, vulgarisms, and professional controversies; and head to the polls on Election Day.

Those who detest him will agonize morning, noon, and night, from this minute until November 3, 2020, desperate to eject him from Washington. That desperation is enormous, all-encompassing. In their view, a Trump loss would signify a restoration of order, balance, decency. A Trump reelection, meanwhile, would portend the death of reason, the end of all that is good in America, and the potential downfall of human civilization.

From the moment Donald Trump was sworn into office on January 20, 2017, his inaugural address an admonitory treatise on "American carnage," I have found myself in countless conversations with voters and political strategists, Democrats and Republicans alike, about Trump's chances for reelection. The consistent, abiding opinion among nearly all of them has been that Trump is the favorite to win in 2020. Some think he is a substantial favorite, no matter whom the Democrats nominate to take him on.

This lack of faith in the Democrats' strategic philosophy and field, and the dearth of optimism from those who want Trump out of office, has been striking. It piqued my professional interest.

Why are so many Democrats convinced that Trump will win four more years? And do the best minds in the party have any idea how to stop him?

I have been covering American politics for over thirty years, and have had the good fortune to meet some of the smartest people in the business. I decided to ask them what they think will be required of the Democratic nominee to actually get those 270 electoral votes and send Trump packing. Over dinners, meetings, telephone discussions, email exchanges, and texts, I sought their expertise and observations, gleaned tricks-of-the-trade insights, and listened to their surefire scenarios and go-for-broke schemes. I asked them all for the unvarnished, fuss-free, straight-talking, no-nonsense, God's-honest, real-news truth.

Few thought beating Trump would be easy. But none thought it impossible. They all had ideas galore.

Trump has some serious weaknesses. His job approval rating has always been a troublesome spot for his administration, despite plenty of good economic news, with loyalty from his core supporters providing an impenetrable floor, but with minimal approbation from the rest of the electorate. Trump has been in extreme negative territory when voters are asked if he has "the personality and leadership qualities a president should have." Both public and private polling have indicated that he is weaker in many of the battleground states than he was when he bested Hillary Clinton.

He also inspires strenuous and conspicuous opposition movements. The earliest days of his term saw the launch of historically large and passionate women's marches around the country and the world. Democrats experienced sweeping victories in the 2018 midterm elections, which had more to do with antipathy toward Trump than with the cyclical nature of politics or the individual contenders themselves. Progressives are gearing up to fight with the same energy and determination now.

But despite Trump's bumpy and shambolic first years in office, there are a number of reasons why so many civilians and campaign consultants think he can be reelected, reasons beyond the political sorcery he utilized in his first run, when he demonstrated a prodigious ability to connect, bully, defy, and sway.

Historically, incumbent presidents just do not lose that often. Since 1900, only four men who won the White House have lost their bids for reelection. By November 2020, it will have been almost thirty years since the American people voted an incumbent out of office.

The press likes to talk about the possibility of loss when a sitting president is challenged because it makes for a good story. In November of 2011, the *New York Times Magazine* ran a cover piece headlined "Is Obama Toast?" declaring that Barack Obama had only a 17 percent chance of winning reelection based on various indicators that previously had been predictive.

Instead, Obama won both the Electoral College, 332 to 206, and the popular vote. The incumbent has advantages, not least of which are mighty money and party apparatuses, fait accompli visuals, an inherent proprietary claim, and the voters' instinctive fear of the unknown. Trump began planning and fundraising for 2020 even before he took office. Whether the Democrats settle on a de facto nominee by March or wait until their national convention in Milwaukee in mid-July, Trump will have had a nearly four-year head start.

The three modern-age presidents who were denied a second term—Gerald Ford, Jimmy Carter, and George H.W. Bush—all faced spirited intra-party challenges for the nomination and saw significant erosion of support within their own parties. Trump will not have to confront those headwinds. He is likely to cruise to renomination and is on a path to receive record backing from Republican voters.

Ford, Carter, and Bush 41, unlike Trump, grappled with severe economic conditions throughout their entire terms. No modern incumbent has lost with a strong economy, and for much of Trump's tenure, the country has seen GDP growth, a rise in productivity and consumer confidence, low inflation, and record low unemployment, including among African Americans and Hispanics. There are, of course, many citizens who have not benefited from the favorable economic conditions, and domestic and global volatility have already demonstrated that the balance can be tilted before Election Day, but Trump still has plenty to jot in his ledger.

The Democratic pollster and strategist Mark Mellman points out that Trump's job approval on the economy in 2019 was higher than his overall job approval rating, a stone's throw from Bill Clinton's comparable number when he won reelection in 1996, and higher than Barack Obama's and George W. Bush's at the same juncture in their successful reelection efforts. Similarly, as Mellman notes, the widely watched University of

Michigan Consumer Sentiment Index has been higher with Trump in the White House than it was for Reagan and Clinton when they were seeking a second term. The economic-based models used by Yale, Moody's, and Trend Macrolytics—all of which have proven track records—have forecasted a Trump victory.

Mellman further observes that the numbers that measure how much voters agree with the president on key issues are not markedly different for Trump than they were for Obama or Bush 43 at this stage.

The Trump administration has been speckled with callous, coarse, and xenophobic policies, sparking domestic anguish and ruffling feathers across the globe. Yet so far, the president has kept the United States out of any new ground wars and has worked to somewhat diminish the American military presence in places such as Iraq and Afghanistan. The optics and execution may be crude, storm clouds may be gathering, but the results to date have translated into relative peace and prosperity.

Trump's slow-burn war with the press also serves him in paradoxical ways. To be sure, elite journalists, collectively, are itching to see Trump fall. Cable television, in particular, churns out a 24/7 chronicle of the outrages of the administration and the man himself, with the story line pleading for his comeuppance.

But the anti-Trump drumbeat in the print media and at CNN and MSNBC begets its own danger. Many Democratic strategists warn that once again the press, as it did four years ago, is creating a distorted impression that Trump cannot win. Throughout the 2016 cycle, the coverage of Trump—from his showman's ride down his gilded escalator to announce his run, to his blustering, unwieldy performances in the debates—was laced with mockery and contempt, building a false confidence that Hillary Clinton, an obviously flawed candidate, was a shoo-in. Some of the voters, who were turned off by both candidates and did not feel like personally casting a ballot for Secretary Clinton, took a pass on the presidential race and then regretted the outcome.

Trump has other advantages as well. Every presidential election is about simultaneously persuading swing voters and inspiring base voters to turn out. One of Trump's biggest political assets is his primal understanding of how to energize the conservative base. By leveraging hot-button issues such as immigration and trade; by demonizing his opponents with cheap nicknames and scurrilous accusations and Fox News screeds and mean tweets; by micro-targeting on social media, Trump and his team know how to get their core voters to the polls. The Democrats might nominate a person who can similarly lather up progressives. But they might not. It is not easy to motivate people to vote against a candidate rather than for a candidate. Just ask Hillary Clinton.

Whatever else one might say about Donald Trump—about his ethics, about his effrontery, about his apparent lack of respect for America's essential values and institutions—the consensus among political strategists is that he is a beast of a competitor. Trump, a former Democrat with no policy or military experience, who had never before run for office of any kind, fought more than a dozen GOP contenders, scooped up forty-one of the fifty-six Republican primary contests, and secured the nomination more easily than any non-incumbent in modern history. He then took on Hillary Clinton, arguably one of the most qualified people ever to seek the Oval Office, and won the presidency.

Yes, Vladimir Putin. Yes, WikiLeaks. Yes, James Comey. Yes, the popular vote. Yes, a lot of other things. But Trump proved victorious when, by conventional standards, he should never have had a chance in the first place. With all due respect to James Carville, forget George W. Bush's reelection in 2004.

Trump's victory in 2016 was the single greatest political achievement of the past several generations.

The strategists I spoke with for this book—many Democrats, but also Republicans who hope Trump is defeated, or who are intrigued by the particular intellectual challenge of this election—have experience working on both winning and losing presidential campaigns. Some currently are involved with 2020 challengers or anti-Trump activist groups. They carry a wide range of personal and professional qualifications, different backgrounds (age, gender, sexual orientation, race, ethnicity), and varied ideological leanings. Some talked on the record, while some insisted on anonymity because they are working for candidates in this election or because of other professional commitments.

All were asked versions of the same fundamental question: What is required to beat Trump on November 3, 2020? They answered this query by drawing on lessons from their past campaigns, by assessing the specific conditions of the 2020 environment, and by analyzing the unique challenges of running against incumbent candidate Trump, the likes of whom no political expert, campaign veteran, or journalist has ever seen before.

Their advice applies to all the Democrats in the field, from the most progressive to the most centrist. Many of the strategists expressed concern that the eventual Democratic nominee will not have the time, inclination, or ability to absorb and execute the kind of ideas presented in this book.

Indeed, the pace of a presidential campaign is breathless, relentless. And, naturally, the first focus must be on the 2020 nominating contest, a fight inevitably so intense that one candidate, Senator Amy Klobuchar, called it a "*Hunger Games* situation." When the Democratic nominee at last emerges from the pile of fellow candidates, victorious but exhausted, she or he will have an urgent, lengthy checklist of things to do, and a campaign treasury likely drained down to pennies.

The White House, meanwhile, will have had plenty of time to build a war chest, settle on a strategy, and define the parameters for the general election season. For the eventual Democratic nominee, clever advice from meddlesome experts will seem like a quaint luxury when the dial has switched from survival mode to flat-out alarm, and the adversary from a pack of starving, frantic wolves to a lone, purring house cat lounging atop an oval cushion stuffed with cash.

Regardless of the pressure, the nominee must pause, regroup, and prepare. A number of the strategists complain that the Clinton campaign never bothered to follow some basic procedures because of the widespread assumption that Secretary Clinton would win the election. But every candidate—novice, veteran, or incumbent—has to be able to answer the single most important question: How, exactly, do I win?

All presidential campaigns are amalgams of art and science, algorithms and handshakes, and successful races are born from many factors. Some are fairly concrete: world events, market fluctuations, and the weather. Others are more nebulous: the mood of the country, fine-spun cultural shifts, even the intuitive and subtle chemistry between candidate and voter. But no factor is more important than what the candidate actually does each day: how she or he reacts to challenges and stresses, reveals personal traits, relates to the audience, avoids or repairs mistakes.

Trump was laughably underestimated by his opponents and most of the media in 2016. Yet virtually every day of his campaign, he successfully defined himself and defined his rivals on his own terms—his greatest skill, and the ultimate key to winning an election. At the time, no one really knew what to make of him. There was frequent speculation that he did not really want the job of president, that his political success was an unwelcome surprise, that his campaign was a PR stunt for his business empire, that he would drop out of the race. Then there was talk that he would not seek reelection.

But Trump always made his goal perfectly clear: he wanted to win. Any other result would stamp him a loser, the label he finds the most humiliating. Being a one-term president also would make him a loser, especially after following three two-termers in Bill Clinton, George W. Bush, and Barack Obama.

So that was, and is, Trump's overarching agenda, his political raison d'etre—to win, and win dirty, if necessary. This does not, naturally, mean his victory is preordained. He most certainly can be beaten, and that event will be determined by the opposition's confidence and ability to design and execute a solid plan. So far, none of the Democratic candidates has demonstrated that he or she knows how to craft a sturdy public image, nor effectively disqualify Trump as a leader. And national and state polls will signify nothing until the incumbent and his challenger actually go one-on-one.

Campaign 2020 will be a doozy. Trump cannot win a referendum, an up-and-down vote, nor a four-more-years blessing, which would be a stretch for most American presidents, not least of all this one. So the president's team will present the election as a choice between two people, focus on ripping the Democrat to shreds, and try to persuade the voters that Trump is the better of two bad options—2016 all over again. Things will get ugly.

To the brave soul who will face that gauntlet, here is advice from the smartest people in politics.

Their collective message: follow these steps if you want the American people to say to Donald Trump those two words he knows so well.

You're fired.

"BEGIN WITH THE END IN MIND."

—STEPHEN COVEY, *THE 7 HABITS OF HIGHLY EFFECTIVE PEOPLE*

WHAT PAUL TULLY KNEW

LESSON: BEATING AN INCUMBENT REQUIRES CONFIDENCE AND A PLAN.

*N*o one pays attention until the conventions.
No one pays attention until Labor Day.
No one pays attention until the closing days of the general election.

So say gaffe-prone candidates, overwhelmed campaign staffers, neurotic journalists, and obsessive news junkies, as they consume and dissect every petty crisis that flares up once a new presidential cycle begins. Sheepishly, they tell each other that real people do not bother about the minutiae of primary campaigns, nor do they pay attention to the trifling daily dramas encountered by freshly minted candidates as they muscle their way through a crowded field. Voters, they opine, will glance through political stories in the paper, eyeball the designated two minutes on the evening news, or casually surf past choice nuggets online, and only really begin to consider the personalities and policies when the contest is in its grand, final swing a few months before Election Day.

This perhaps was once true, but only in part. The majority of voters, certainly, have never cared who aces the Iowa

Jefferson-Jackson dinner or scores the endorsement of some wizened former cabinet secretary. But they pick up data on the issues and missteps that matter to them, and those impressions stick. And, of course, for the candidates, early successes elevate fundraising, media interest, mojo, and momentum, news of which trickles down to all but the most blasé citizens.

Now, with 21st-century social media, every blunder can be handily resurrected and registered anew. One well-placed link to a thirty-second clip on YouTube, and the past becomes the present. No one understands this better than Twitter devotee Donald Trump. The master of defining his rivals knows exactly how to highlight a blooper, cement an unpalatable trait, fashion a damning meme. Twitter has changed the game, especially when utilized by a bored president with no filter and zero impulse control.

The truth is, good planning has always been essential to a winning campaign, never more so than today. It may have seemed as if Trump entered the race on a lark and winged it until the White House. But he had a clear and specific formula—taking out his opposition one by one, the order determined by who most threatened him in the polls, while simultaneously keeping Hillary Clinton in his sights and defining her on his terms.

He also had supreme confidence that he could execute his strategy and execute his rivals. To be sure, Trump himself occasionally doubted he could actually win the presidency. But he projected such brashness, such certainty, that victory became a self-fulfilling prophecy, first for his campaign team and then for his voters.

This potent equation—a cocksure candidate with a viable plan—boosted him as a political force and greased his way with the GOP. His method was effective both practically and psychologically.

Confidence and strategy were vital to Trump, and they are even more vitally important when trying to wrest control of the White House from a sitting president.

The last person to beat an incumbent was Bill Clinton. Clinton, of course, had yearned to be president from his youth, and had crafted his entire professional life to that end. The name of the Arkansas town in which he was born—Hope—was what he inspired in his home-state constituents, and what he had in abundance when it came to his own ambitions. By 1991, Governor Clinton was champing to seize the crown and was wise enough to seek help wherever he could find it. In June of that year, Clinton hunkered down on a lush estate in Virginia surrounded by meticulously groomed gardens and paddocks, listening to a pitch about how to dislodge George H.W. Bush from the White House.

And now his hope had a plan.

• • •

Middleburg, Virginia, is horse country. It is a rarified combination of old money, Southern sensibility, and 18th-century historic charm, yet it lies just an hour west of Washington, D.C. Willow Oaks, a country manor nestled in the lower tier of Loudoun County, had been purchased by Averell Harriman, heir to the Union Pacific Railroad and Wells Fargo fortunes, governor of New York, presidential candidate, and esteemed elder statesman. He had bought the estate as a gift for his wife.

Pamela Digby Churchill Hayward Harriman, the daughter of British aristocrats, was one of the most influential political players of the twentieth century. In 1939, at the age of nineteen, she wed Randolph Churchill, son of Winston Churchill. The marriage was brief, and for the next three decades, she led a glittering life romancing and being romanced by a who's who of the era's most famous and powerful men. She married Averell Harriman, her third husband, in 1971, became an American citizen, and launched her career as a Democratic activist.

After the party lost both the White House and the Senate majority in 1980, Pamela Harriman formed a political action committee, "Democrats for the '80s," eventually nicknamed "PamPac." She held big-dollar fundraisers and served as an advisor to a variety of prominent groups. She knew most everyone in the party firmament, but Bill Clinton was one of her favorites. He was on the board of her PAC, and the two acted as mutual sounding boards.

The salons Harriman hosted in her Georgetown town house were the stuff of legend, and continued long after Averell's death in 1986. Harriman also regularly gathered powerful friends and comrades at the Willow Oaks estate. And so it was on June 13, 1991, that the high guard of the party convened a two-day "Middleburg meeting" to present a strategy to win back the Oval Office the following year.

To most of those invited, the prospect seemed dim. With the exception of Jimmy Carter's blighted four years after Watergate, the party had been shut out of the White House since 1968. Republicans were consistently sweeping mega-states such as California, Michigan, Ohio, Texas, Florida, and New Jersey as part of a seemingly impregnable Electoral College Lock, rendering the chance of a successful Democratic presidential campaign a long shot. Bush had won a smashing victory in the Gulf War against Saddam Hussein in February, and had seen his approval rating soar above 90 percent at the beginning of 1991, compounding the difficulty.

It was the Democratic National Committee's chairman, Ron Brown, who called the Middleburg meeting. Brown, a longtime party activist, was born in Washington, D.C., and raised in Harlem, where he enjoyed a sophisticated, prep school upbringing. After the army and law school, he toggled between roles as a political advisor and elite law firm lobbyist, until he won the job as the chief DNC operative in a competitive race after Massachusetts governor Michael Dukakis was handily beaten by Bush and the party demanded new leadership. The group Brown took over was broke and directionless.

Although Brown had supported the progressive candidacy of Jesse Jackson in 1988, his ties were deep and broad throughout the party. He knew and lived the first rule of politics: you cannot govern if you do not win.

Urbane and unflappable, Brown was determined to erect the foundations of a forceful campaign, even if President Bush appeared strong and the Democratic Party lacked an obvious frontrunner. Many of the biggest names in the Democratic constellation were said to be considering the race—much of the speculation centered on New York governor Mario Cuomo—but none had yet committed.

Well aware that a party nominee would not be selected any time soon, Brown worked with his team and with Harriman to first strengthen the DNC itself, building a more engaged and aggressive operation. He planned to bolster and invigorate the state parties, train campaign workers nationwide, and personally serve as the party's primary spokesperson, vigorously denouncing Bush's policies and record, especially on the economy. He needed to set the stage for a fierce Democratic Party that could properly support a feasible candidate, and to that end, his main order of business was to empower and unleash Paul Tully.

Tully, the national committee's chief political strategist, had worked in every presidential election since 1968, rising to increasingly senior positions, although he was not well known outside the tightest circles of the party. In the pre-Internet age, such people—wickedly smart, highly influential, profoundly inspirational—could still remain anonymous to the general public. Chances are that most of the people running for president in 2020 and most of the readers of this book have never heard of Tully.

But he was a singular figure in the 1992 campaign and beloved by his Democratic allies. "Pacing, driven, and full of joy," as Ron Brown described him, Tully's mission was to take Democrats who were cynical, skeptical, and hopeless and turn them into believers. He assured his party brethren that President Bush, despite his astronomical approval ratings and the Democrats' losing streak, could in fact be voted out of the White House.

Tully, a tireless evangelist, gave an endless succession of briefings all over D.C. and the country. He spoke at party headquarters, donor retreats, strategist powwows, union groups, and meetings of congressional members, with the purpose of rallying them all to action. A rumpled bear of a man with big appetites, he chain-smoked Pall Mall cigarettes, drank vodka by the liter, and usually sported the remnants of a gobbled meal on his beat-up Oxford shirt or ratty tie. When he spoke, his tousled dark hair flopped over his forehead, his sausage-fingered hands waved frantically, and his arms extended like pointers to drive home an idea. He kept his eyeglasses tied to a string around his neck, resting on his chest, or perched on the end of his nose, making him look, his friends teased, like a little old lady. In fact, for all his brashness and swagger, Tully displayed a soft inner side that enhanced the humanity his friends found so appealing. Like his boss Ron Brown, he cared about what the party stood for, but his job was to help Democrats win.

Tully was a champion of data and graphics when those mechanisms were still in their infancy in politics. His insights were tailor-made for the digital age, but he worked with the rudimentary tools available to him at the time—acetate transparencies displayed on overhead projectors, personal encyclopedic knowledge, and great storytelling.

One of Tully's gifts was the ability to communicate complicated ideas through tales and yarns, like the one about the South Philadelphia congressman who had built up such a bond walking the streets of his district over the years that he won reelection even though he died a few weeks before Election Day. Tully would apply uncluttered analogies to everyday activities.

"Why do you go to a movie?" he'd ask rhetorically. Then he would answer his own question. "You go to a movie because you like the actress or the actor, or you go to a movie because you like action." Then he would walk his audience through a complex political strategy or thorny campaign decision in a manner that was similarly relatable.

Tully, along with his colleague Mark Steitz, worked with data guru Mark Gersh to update the presentation constantly, so he could include in his road show the latest figures identifying the battleground state voters he was sure could be successfully swayed in order to get to a winning 270 electoral votes.

As James Carville once said, "Tully had every map, every target. He probably knew the name of every swing voter in the country." Tully's goals were to persuade candidates and donors that victory was possible and to help the party prepare a solid battle plan for the general election, a plan that would be handed over to the nominee once the bruising primaries and caucuses were over. Tully's thesis was streamlined, resourceful, and easy to follow.

Politics is always in motion, Tully would say. *You are always either moving up or moving down. If you can't explain conclusively why you are moving up, then you are moving down.*

Ron Brown and his team needed an infusion of cash to execute Tully's strategy, so he and Harriman hatched a scheme.

To lure the party's biggest donors to a meeting and prompt them to open their checkbooks, they would use as bait some of the most-talked-about Democratic elected officials, including possible presidential candidates. Most of the contributors were trying to figure out which horse to back, and gathering the top 1992 prospects at Willow Oaks, with shared meals and conversations and working sessions, would treat the fat cats to some special access.

Brown and Harriman knew that few of the potential candidates would turn down such an invitation; Harriman could make or break a politician's career, and she was not used to hearing "no" from the powerful. Just as the contributors relished rubbing shoulders with the pols, for those considering a challenge to Bush, this was an unparalleled opportunity to impress potential major backers of a presidential campaign. There is nothing more appealing to a candidate who is considering a major political undertaking than access to cash.

At the meeting, only former Massachusetts senator Paul Tsongas had officially entered the race, while Clinton and Senators Tom Harkin of Iowa and Bob Kerrey of Nebraska were expected to soon announce their bids. Others in attendance with presidential ambitions included Missouri congressman Dick Gephardt, New Jersey senator Bill Bradley, and West Virginia senator Jay Rockefeller. Willow Oaks also was hosting Texas senator Lloyd Bentsen, who had been Dukakis' running mate; Speaker of the House Tom Foley of Washington State; and Senator George Mitchell of Maine.

Invitees who had sent their regrets included Tennessee senator Al Gore, Virginia governor Douglas Wilder, civil rights activist and former presidential candidate Jesse Jackson, and, most significantly, Governor Cuomo, whom many in the party considered the frontrunner-in-waiting.

Harriman had assembled about two dozen major contributors, women and men who were interested and invested in the health of the party and its issues agenda, and were reliably generous givers. They were not dilettantes but the backbone of the Democratic elite, true believers in the goals and values of the party. They were skeptical that Bush could be beaten, but were open to the pitch.

Among them were Walter Shorenstein, Penny Pritzker, Shelia Davis Lawrence, Monte Friedkin, Steve Grossman, Elizabeth Frawley Bagley, Barry Diller, Peter Lewis, Edgar Bronfman, Jr., Al Checchi, Michael Del Giudice, Ted Field, Richard Dennis, Alida Rockefeller Messinger, Hugh Westbrook, and Phil Angelides. This was in the era before social media, and the Democrats had been locked out of the White House for so long that even the party's most prominent donors, who lived all around the country, in many cases did not know each other well. Some had never met before. This was an extraordinary opportunity to get Democratic money and candidates on the same page.

As one of Brown's top advisors put it, *Martin Luther King said, "I have a dream," not "I have a plan."* Brown needed both. He needed the party to dream big, to imagine that victory was possible, so that it would head into the general election with the confidence required to beat the incumbent. It was basic psychology: *you cannot win unless you think you can win.* Brown also knew that the donors, strategists, party officials, and politicians at the Harriman estate were a seasoned and realistic group. The DNC team had to take this opportunity to sell these realists on the logic of dreaming. It was an assemblage that was unprecedented in modern political history and has never been precisely replicated by either party since.

"Ron, how do you do this?" one of his staff members asked him just a few weeks before Middleburg. "How do you exude this optimism in the face of every ounce of evidence to the contrary?"

"It's my job," Brown replied.

• • •

Dukakis' loss had left the party in shambles, but he had bequeathed one important legacy to the DNC. His finance guy, Bob Farmer, had increased so-called soft-money donations, large checks from individuals that could be made available for party-building activities and coordinated campaigns with state operations to benefit the presidential ticket.

After Dukakis became the party's de facto nominee in the spring of 1988, Farmer got many of the party's most generous contributors to pony up giant gifts, often at the $100,000 level or above—perfectly legal but a stunning amount at the time. This money was immensely important for the Democrats, who were overall at a financial disadvantage. They were badly outraised by the Republicans, who were particularly adept at raking in small contributions through direct mail solicitations.

After Brown assumed the chairmanship, his top aide, Rob Stein, looked at the quarter-by-quarter contributions the party had drawn in the previous presidential cycle and noticed that far too much of the money came in at the very end of the quadrennial process, after a nominee had been selected. The cash was always desperately needed, but it arrived too late to be used to build the bedrock of the general election campaign. Stein and his colleagues understood the donors' rationale—why give a large sum to a disorganized party before a nominee was chosen, when one might give a splashy figure at the end and snag an ambassadorship or a White House sleepover as a personal thank-you?

But Tully's plan needed funding right away. He had to collect research on general election voters and build the coordinated campaigns with the states. His team estimated it would require about three million dollars, which was serious money back then. Brown believed it was essential that Tully get going as soon as possible.

That is where Harriman came in. Stein and his colleagues devised the Middleburg meeting to bring together the top donors with the top politicians, and let them feel they were all part of something special, something momentous, something so authentically designed and beautifully executed that the Democrats would take back the White House no matter who they nominated. In other words, a dream with a plan.

Brown's team—Stein, Alexis Herman, Melissa Moss, Bob Burkett—knew the meeting was a roll of the dice. They decided to give the attendees only the scantest information about the agenda in advance. They had no idea if Tully's proposal would satisfy, if the donors would write checks, if the candidates would be willing to cede some autonomy to the DNC. What they did know was that if Middleburg failed, there was no Plan B.

The DNC team labored over the logistics—donors and politicians were traveling in from all over the country, had to be housed in pleasant accommodations, and then be treated to a real show at a real showplace. The whole event had to be exceptional, memorable, unique. The number of attendees had to be large enough for the financial objectives to be accomplished but small enough for the mood to be seductively intimate.

The guests, who had been culled and curated, had all attended countless prestigious events and visited countless fancy houses. They were used to mingling with powerful, famous, wealthy people. They were powerful, famous, and wealthy themselves. Willow Oaks satisfied as a venue, Pamela Harriman as a hostess. There was not a soul on the guest list, jaded or otherwise, who would be unswayed by a pedigree and biography that included earls, barons, mavericks, Winston Churchill, Edward R. Murrow, Élie de Rothschild, Frank Sinatra, and two decades of political kingmaking.

The organizers worked with the political staff to coach their principals on how to interact with the donors. *Treat them as peers. No showing off. No self-important lectures or speeches.* They wanted to create a vibe of inclusion and equipoise, people coming together for a common mission, not a networking opportunity.

•　　•　　•

On the afternoon of June 13, Harriman, in her lush, aristocratic voice, welcomed the group, about four dozen in all. They were seated around her spacious living room in a wide circle, on roomy sofas and comfortable chairs, fine art on the walls, imposing glass doors leading to surrounding rooms. A number of those in attendance had been to Willow Oaks before; the estate was sometimes jokingly referred to as the "Southern headquarters of the DNC." For others, it was their first visit, and they were duly enthralled. It was an idyllic setting, with understated, pastoral elegance suggesting a physical and even chronological distance from the modern worlds of business and politics that were represented there.

Harriman, plummy and gracious, thanked her guests for coming and reminded them of the stakes of the next election. The room was hushed; Harriman's involvement alone added substance to the proceedings, as well as glamour. If she had confidence in the DNC's plan, her guests were willing to listen. She kept things short and Brown stepped up.

The chairman normally favored expensively tailored suits, but he was dressed casually for this meeting. It was his intention that the event feel like an informal gathering of friends and family, not a stuffy business session. Already he held the admiration of these leading Democrats; in his years as chair, he had impressed them as an honest broker. He just wanted to win, and so did they.

The guests as a whole appeared to be in the proper frame of mind, which delighted and reassured the members of the

DNC staff. The donors all seemed well settled and attentive, and there was no preening or posturing or secret plotting from the 1992 aspirants. The prospective candidates were there to support Ron Brown's agenda rather than advance their own, well aware that no one had a chance at winning the White House if the DNC was not rebuilt.

Brown skipped over perfunctory greetings and Pollyannaish clichés. Instead, he asked everyone in the room, even the boldfaced names and icons, to introduce themselves. When that was done, Brown spoke for an hour, delivering individually crafted homages to every donor and politician present. It was a captivating performance. Moving about the sumptuous space, Brown recounted stories about how he had originally met each person, or how he had been impressed by their words or insights, or how he had seen them do something heroic, or generous, or exceptional. It was clear his approach was effective. The atmosphere glowed and grew warm with pride and pleasure.

Brown reached Walter Shorenstein. The cantankerous and taciturn San Francisco billionaire was sitting with his arms folded, displaying his signature expression of impassivity and mild boredom. Brown turned on the charm, showering the real estate developer with effusive, perceptive praise. Shorenstein opened up like a flower, a gratified smile crossing his face.

Brown's message was clear. Not one of us can pull this off alone. Not one of us can succeed without help. We need a shared conviction we can win and a shared plan that will allow us to win. Implicit in his words: we need the resources to put that plan into effect. Bush could be beaten, he said plainly. Sure, the president was riding high, his poll numbers daunting. But those levels of support were transitory. These are Bush's best days politically, Brown told the crowd. If they were willing to invest in the party, they could all embark together on a historic journey, and seize back the White House as a team.

Brown was impassioned, but also transactional and matter-of-fact. Of course everyone there wanted to serve a higher purpose and believed in the values of the Democratic Party. But what was on the agenda here was cold hard cash.

Brown made it clear that their plan for beating Bush required more soft money than the DNC had on hand. He needed the donors to come up with several million dollars to invest in the infrastructure required to get things ready for the eventual nominee. It could not wait. It had to happen immediately.

Then it was Paul Tully's turn. Tully had been informed he would have to do an abbreviated version of his presentation, about twenty minutes total. Every one of his numbers, every one of his slides, was precious to him, so he labored to choose just the right components to include. He had to convince the donors that their money would go to good use. He knew they would understand the concept of coordinated campaigns in battleground states and the search for swing voters, so he emphasized those elements of the plan.

Tully viewed his presentations as performance, himself as an actor, and he suffered terrible stage fright. Before he started speaking, he would pace into a perspiring, nervous lather, continue pacing and dripping when his lecture began, and emerge drenched in sweat by the time he was finished. But he had a receptive audience at Willow Oaks. Harriman's estate was unquestionably ornate and overstuffed, yet she made it cozy, livable, and the guests were comfortable, engaged, and primed.

Clinton was especially rapt as Tully brought forth the case he had been peddling since 1989, that Bush was beatable if the right Democrat with the right message targeted the right voters in the right states. Dukakis might have lost badly, but Tully looked at the changes that had occurred over just a few years, such as the massive growth in the suburbs, and saw the possibilities for his party.

There are two kinds of presidential candidates, Tully told them—those who can count and those who lose. Although he displayed an array of Gersh's data to make his points, in the end, Tully intoned, there were really only two numbers that mattered: the number of delegates at the convention necessary to achieve a majority and the number of electoral votes necessary to claim the White House.

One of the challenges, Tully explained, was that candidates seeking the nomination had to spend an inordinate amount of time wooing voters to win delegates in states that would not matter in the general election. The key was to find a way through surrogates, travel, paid media, television appearances, radio broadcasts, and a consistent message to begin reaching out to voters as early as possible. Then the party would be in a position to judiciously cobble together the best combination of states to get the 270 electoral votes required to beat Bush.

The slides shifted one by one. Tully gestured to the data, spitting out words and phrases punctuated by his New York accent and an occasional grunt, as the images changed. His friends called him the most inarticulate articulate person they had ever met.

Pay.

Wages, all right?

Going down, okay?

You got it, you got it, you got it?

Costs up . . . Health care, okay, okay.

There is all this, right?

Just, like, worried about the future.

Tully saw the possibility of a new, emerging Democratic majority based on the nation's changing economic order that could allow the party to pick the Electoral College Lock in 1992, even if it could not yet smash it. While complacent Republicans and downtrodden Democrats thought Bush would ride incumbency and his national security record to reelection,

Tully believed the economy would eventually develop as the bigger issue. "This is about money in my pocket, prices for the essentials of life, the level of fear on the block," Tully asserted several months later, when the election was a year away.

Open your wallets, Tully instructed the donors in Middleburg. Your money will be well spent.

Get off the fence, he urged the prospective candidates. Get into the race.

Tully batted away every perceived obstacle: the complacency of the electorate, the reverberations of the Reagan Revolution, Bush's apparent triumph in the Gulf War, and his 90 percent approval rating when it ended. Tully talked about Clement Attlee, saying that Attlee beat Churchill in 1945 as World War II was coming to a close because the populace was shifting toward domestic, personal concerns. Tully assessed the current economic situation, a precursor to James Carville's famous "It's the economy, stupid," to explain how the Democrats could use the conditions to influence voters.

After a polling presentation from Mark Mellman and a casual dinner, the guests dispersed to their inns and hotel rooms. There was a hum of excitement and apperception. Something major was happening. The donors were asking thoughtful, canny questions. The presidential hopefuls had indicated they would give their wholehearted support to the nominee. Brown and Tully had convinced them the Democrats could win back the White House. As long as they all worked together.

• • •

The next morning, the guests were divided into groups, five or six donors paired off with one prospective presidential candidate or congressional leader. They were placed in different locations around the estate; given tall, standing easels draped with large sheets of paper; and instructed to review the information they had heard from Brown, Tully, and Mellman the previous day, adding thoughts and insights as they dissected the data and brainstormed fresh ideas. A DNC facilitator was present to take notes and keep the conversations and dynamics on track.

Clinton's group was assigned to an outdoor seating area, and its members discussed the plan for over an hour. At the breakout session, as he had the day before, Clinton adhered to the rules, tamping down his natural allure and instinct for attracting the spotlight. But even in his understated mode, he wowed the donors, including some who had been leaning toward Kerrey or Harkin. Many were encountering Bill Clinton for the first time, and years later, they still recalled being dazzled. The rules for Middleburg had been explicit. The meeting was not about settling on a candidate for 1992. But one contender inevitably stood out.

The guests reconvened for a farewell buffet lunch, and the anticipatory hum of the previous night had strengthened into a buzz. The compelling analyses and debates that sprung up during the breakout sessions had made the Democrats even more confident that Brown and Tully's plan—agile, astute, audacious—could be effective, and had further bonded them as a group.

As the guests were finishing up their lunch, the DNC team finally made the ask. We need three million dollars to execute the plan we have been discussing, they told the donors. They requested at least $100,000 from each person in attendance.

Monte Friedkin, a longtime contributor from Florida, felt the urgency to act before everyone scattered, leaving DNC staffers to beg for checks in strained, follow-up telephone appeals. Unprompted, he leaped forward and took the floor with a call to arms. It was a moment some of the Yiddish-speaking Jewish donors in Middleburg would call "tuchus oyfn tish"— *put your ass on the table*. It was time for the party's biggest financial backers to put their asses on the table and open their wallets.

We've been here now for a day, said Friedkin. *We need to get one thing done. I don't think any of us can walk out of this room without making a specific pledge for a significant investment in the party. If we can give Ron the money he needs to invest in infrastructure, then we can create a transformative moment.* He stood back, ready to write his own check.

The DNC staff in the room exchanged looks, restrained but unmistakable: *Holy shit.* They proceeded to get commitments of nearly one and a half million dollars right there and then, over the next few weeks, would raise a comparable amount, reaching the three-million-dollar goal to finance Tully's plan.

The Middleburg meeting was coming to a close, but Ron Brown had one final piece of business on the docket. He led a delegation of donors and elected officials down a steep hill to greet a throng of national political reporters. The press had been fascinated by the gathering—the venue, the handful of names that had escaped the guest list, the unprecedented nature of candidates and bigwigs having such a palaver—and the DNC wanted to project a show of force. It seemed to those who attended the Middleburg meeting that the experience could be monumentally consequential, although the details—donors contributing hefty checks to support Tully's plan; candidates promising unity; considerable coordination between the DNC and the nominee's campaign—would stay largely confidential.

Ron Brown reached the bottom of the slope and surveyed the journalists. "Evidently there's been some interest in what's been going on up the hill."

Brown gave the reporters a gilded summary, without disclosing the key specifics. "We have had an extraordinary meeting," he said, "a historic meeting for the Democratic Party.

There was absolute consensus that we're on the right track, getting ready for the 1992 general election campaign early on. George Bush is very vulnerable in 1992 because this administration has absolutely no domestic agenda.

"We've developed a strategy," he continued, "a preliminary strategy for the 1992 general election campaign. The essence of it is to have our party leaders and our prospective candidates and our national party working together as a team. There is consensus, and that teamwork has started as of today. The kind of unanimity, the kind of spirit, the kind of positive feeling and optimism about the future that was exhibited both today and yesterday astonished even those of us who are responsible for pulling this meeting together."

"What's your strategy?" a reporter called out.

"Well, actually, you know, when you have a strategy, you keep it to yourself because you have adversaries. But the strategy has been shared very clearly with the leadership here today. They support it. We know that we've got to run a much more sophisticated campaign than the Democratic Party has run in the past. It's got to be tough, hard-nosed, a professional operation. We've got to do the kind of research and polling and focus-group work and message testing and voter outreach that we haven't been prepared to do in the past."

Brown sketched the basics. "We all understand that getting the nomination is only the first phase. The important thing is to win a general election . . . and have the opportunity to create the kind of atmosphere of change that we need in America, to get our country back on the right track. You have to get an early start. You can't wait until your party's nominating convention is over before you start thinking about general election planning and strategy."

The session was opened to more questions. Gwen Ifill of the *New York Times* was interested in hearing from the man from Hope. "Governor Clinton, if you were to run for president, could you win on this secret strategy that you all were talking about?" she asked.

"I believe that the research confirms what any workaday politician would find who went out and just talked to real people," Clinton replied. "That they have real problems, real concerns. They don't think they're being addressed at the national level. And if we can come up with a message that brings people together around these concerns, then the Democrats have a chance to win in '92."

Warming to his message, Clinton continued. "Working people are making less money and working longer hours and spending less time with their kids than they were ten years ago. They're worried sick, thirty-something million of them, when they go to work, their kids are going to get sick and they won't be able to pay the bills. And they don't have any clue about how they're going to educate 'em. They're worried that their schools aren't very good, and when they get out they won't be able to afford to send them to college. That's what they're worried about, and they know that that is depressing the economic strength of this country and our long-term future. That's what the core problems of the country are. That's what the Democrats have always been concerned about and that's why we feel pretty good about the prospects of making a real contribution in '92."

• • •

By year's end, Clinton, Harkin, and Kerrey joined Tsongas in the race, along with Governor Wilder and California governor Jerry Brown. Many of the bigger names, including Cuomo, passed, daunted by Bush's advantages and the historical fact that, other than Jimmy Carter, the most recent elected incumbent president to fall short in a bid for a second term was Herbert Hoover.

Tully and Brown kept up their efforts through the summer, fall, and winter of 1991, and continued into 1992. Bill Clinton announced his candidacy in October of 1991, and bounded off on his chaotic, twisting path to victory. When Clinton at last arrived at the nomination, badly damaged politically and with little money in the bank—largely due to his own history and foibles—Tully took up residence at the Little Rock campaign headquarters, working side by side with James Carville, George Stephanopoulos, and the other members of Clinton's high command, using his data to target voters down to the precinct level in the battleground states.

Team Clinton, like its candidate, was optimistic about his chances, but many of its members retained nagging doubts that Bush could be beaten. Tully, however, remained buoyantly confident, and, along with Chairman Brown, Gersh, and other colleagues, convinced legions of Democrats that the Republican incumbent could be unseated. He continued to update and scrutinize his data, and by late September 1992, with just over a month until Election Day, saw some promising signs. Bush had suddenly pulled all of his television advertising off of California stations, conceding the state, and Tully thought this was a decisive tell.

On September 23, Tully strolled into the Little Rock headquarters with a new statistic. "This thing is 85 percent done," he said. He walked around the space repeating the phrase over and over, to everyone he encountered. A Clinton win, he believed, was now a high probability.

Some of the staffers in the headquarters were unnerved by his cheerful certainty and felt it was premature, that he was tempting fate. But others, bone-tired and emotionally fraught, thought to themselves, *Tully just might be right about all this, okay?*

Two days later, on September 25, a maid entered the Little Rock hotel room Tully had been calling home since spring and discovered his inert body. The local coroner determined he had died of a heart attack, at age forty-eight. The Clinton team was shocked, devastated, bereft. Tully passed away before he was able to see his prediction of a Clinton victory come true, and before he was able to get the credit he deserved for his role. Today, Democrats who knew Tully speak about him with reverence. A number of people contributed to Bill Clinton's historic victory. But Tully's combination of data, intensity, and confidence was indispensable.

There is no Paul Tully in the Democratic Party today. No one at the Democratic National Committee serves that function, and after charges of favoritism toward Hillary Clinton four years ago, such a collaboration would only cause trouble. Under current election law, no outside advocacy group is positioned to step in and provide that same help.

The strategists who were interviewed for this book said Tully's approach was an invaluable blueprint for a winning campaign; that every candidate should examine what Tully accomplished, consider the principles behind his method, and execute as much of the strategy as possible themselves.

This will be a Herculean task. The rash, capricious Trump is a far different animal than was George H. W. Bush, who played by old-school political rules of engagement and decorum. For all this steely acumen and hard experience, Bush was a gentleman to the bone who favored governing over campaigning. It will be a heavy load indeed to trounce a large covey of Democratic rivals and tangle with Trump, without anyone like Tully, Brown, and the 1992 team managing the legwork and deciphering the electoral brain teasers.

Paul Tully provided a wise, informed, singular voice promising answers and results. *We can beat this powerful incumbent*, he said, *and here's how*.

What Democrats lacked in 2019 and will lack for many more months is a singular voice of reason and clarity. What they have instead is a cacophony of clamoring candidates and staffers and party leaders, each with unique ideas about how to fight and win. A successful candidate will have to find a reservoir of absolute confidence that Trump can be beaten, no matter what instinct, fear, statistics, and the chattering class suggest.

• • •

But the paradox remains. Candidates in the Democratic field will have to spend every waking minute, through at least March and possibly through July, focusing all of their mental and physical resources on winning the nomination. If they take an eye off that ball, a general election strategy becomes moot. But if they do not spend some effort starting in the winter thinking about how to beat Donald Trump, a nomination win becomes immaterial.

The biggest mistake a candidate can make, the strategists say, is to fail to take the necessary and available steps to prepare for the endgame. On the Republican side, Trump and his reelection campaign will be barreling along every day, raising money, testing versions of Facebook ads, and identifying, profiling, analyzing, and mobilizing a general election electorate. The Democratic opponents must explain their political motivations, avoid squabbles, and rack up primary wins, but be ready to pivot cleanly from the tumult of delegates and Democratic voters to the challenges of the Electoral College and general election voters.

"Begin with the end in mind," says Jill Alper, a Michigan-based strategist who worked for the Clinton-Gore team and John Kerry, quoting the famous axiom by Stephen Covey. "The best way to win the primary is to talk about Donald Trump. Right? And the best way to win the general election is to talk about Donald Trump. So how do you talk about Donald Trump to achieve those objectives at the same time?" In a way, a winning candidate must run a campaign that is a palindrome of sorts, one that reveals brain and soul and skill, that lives in the moment, in the daily struggles, but holds November 2020 close. The candidate should maintain personal consistency, a steady message, and true principles, from start to finish, finish to start.

So the questions to the candidates persist:

In the harsh chill of winter, can you, with confidence, synchronously make the best strategic and tactical choices to win 1,885 delegates and 270 electoral votes? Can you work backwards from Election Day and do what is required to oust Trump?

According to the people interviewed for this book, not only can you, you must. As Will Robinson, a longtime colleague of Tully's, says, "The campaign to beat Donald Trump is not a one-day sale." It is a long-term crusade that requires a plan and a backbone worthy of Ron Brown and Paul Tully.

And it starts right now, say the strategists. Find your own voice, break free from the pack, but make it a top priority to understand both the man you want to replace and the citizens who gave him the job in the first place.

PART I
WINTER

"WINTER IS NOT A SEASON,
IT'S AN OCCUPATION."
—SINCLAIR LEWIS

CHAPTER ONE
THE MOVEMENT

LESSON: UNDERSTAND
DONALD TRUMP AND HIS VOTERS.

At 4 PM on September 20th, 2016, a little more than six weeks before Election Day, Donald Trump's private plane touched down on the single runway of Albert J. Ellis Airport in Richlands, North Carolina. Richlands, so named because of the quality of the soil, was the first town in Onslow County to have both its own library and museum. In 2016, its population was about 1,500 souls.

Donald Trump exited the plane, was loaded by his Secret Service and staff into his motorcade, and traveled thirty minutes to Kenansville, an even smaller town, with a population of 847, for a rally that evening at the Duplin County Event Center. The venue had previously hosted monster truck exhibitions, high school graduations, wrestling tournaments, and an animal charity showcase where prizes included "cash, jewelry, and guns."

As the motorcade made its way through the bucolic countryside, the campaign staff and traveling press corps noticed the traffic was particularly heavy for a late-afternoon Tuesday in such a sparsely populated rural area.

When Trump arrived shortly before 5 PM, he found over ten thousand people outside the event center, with thousands more inside, waiting for him. He gave a version of his Mr.-Trump's-Wild-Ride stump speech, hitting many of his favorite themes: Mexico, China, immigration, the vile media, corrupt Hillary Clinton, and the rigged election system. "And we know it's a rigged system," Trump said. "All you have to do is ask Bernie Sanders and you'll see."

Trump offered a few screeds of fresh material, slamming President Obama and the conditions in urban areas. "Our African American communities are absolutely in the worst shape that they've ever been in before, ever, ever, ever," he thundered. "You take a look at the inner cities, you get no education, you get no jobs, you get shot walking down the street. They're worse. I mean, honestly, places like Afghanistan are safer than some of our inner cities."

Trump's rhetoric in Kenansville was shocking and offensive, but it was not out of character. The rally was much like his other arena performances—raucous and caustic, replete with grim warnings, exultant boasts, and nasty riffs, yet infused with a winking, jovial intimacy. Some observers wondered why Trump would burn valuable time during the final weeks of the campaign in the backwoods of North Carolina. Most Democrats just dismissed his speech as typical, tacky Trump.

But the rally itself was a classic example of how Trump won the presidency. Duplin County turned out to be one of the year's most significant events. By going to an out-of-the-way part of a battleground state, drawing a massive, enthusiastic crowd, and spending time with rural and farm voters who rarely get to see a presidential candidate in person, let alone at such a critical juncture in the campaign, Trump sent the message that the members of his movement deserved to be heard, even in—especially in—the most remote parts of the country.

Beneath the radar, word got around in conservative networks that Trump had done something extraordinary. Three thousand miles away in California, the Republican mother of Michigan's former Democratic governor, Jennifer Granholm, heard about the location of the rally and how many farmers and other rural folks had turned out. She told her daughter, a strong backer of Hillary Clinton, how remarkable it was. While not a Trump supporter herself, Granholm's mother knew how affecting it must have been for those Republicans in North Carolina. "If you are coming here," they felt, "it means we matter."

Trump had sent up a clear signal that traveled well beyond Kenansville. In his words, he was truly leading a movement, and his campaign was listening to "the forgotten men and women" of the United States.

* * *

In many ways, Donald Trump is a simple man to understand. His ego, a colossal, all-encompassing beast, is his guiding force. He exhibits little curiosity about the world at large, except how it relates to him. This, in part, explains his rapport with some of the world's most ruthless, notorious, and malignant dictators. When praised by Vladimir Putin, Trump said, "It is always a great honor to be so nicely complimented by a man so highly respected within his own country and beyond." Trump and North Korea's Kim Jong-un, meanwhile, bonded the old-fashioned way, through courtship by pen. "He wrote me beautiful letters," Trump said. "And they are great letters. We fell in love." Trump regularly restates this mutual affection. "I like him, he likes me. I guess that's okay. Am I allowed to say that?" Kim Jong-un also received Trump's awed affirmation as a murderous badass. "He goes in, he takes over, and he's the boss," Trump exclaimed. "It's incredible. He wiped out the uncle. He wiped out this one, that one. I mean, this guy doesn't play games."

Trump's susceptibility to flattery, and its reverse—a scalding fury at censure—extends to the president's interactions with friends, business associates, political colleagues, and acquaintances. Every comment becomes personal, albeit from a one-sided perspective, and every transaction a quid pro quo, although he often demands the quid and ignores the quo. Born into great wealth, offered every advantage, rarely held accountable for his actions or prompted to show gratitude or grace, endlessly rewarded (bankruptcies notwithstanding) for his outsized dreams and gleeful greed (building contracts, global branding, icon status, TV stardom, household fame, the White House), Trump has never faced cold, hard consequences for his baser acts and grasping profligacy. The result? An arrogant, eccentric, isolated, fragile, vain, obdurate narcissist. It is all quite straightforward, and his formula applies to absolutely everyone. (Except, of course, to his daughter Ivanka.) Say something nice about Trump, and he is charmed and pacified. Criticize him, even in the mildest, limited, innocuous way, and feel his wrath, whether it be a 280-character Twitter attack or a lifelong feud. One is either friend or foe, and the phrase "what have you done for me lately?" is always applicable.

But to fathom why he is such a talented presidential candidate takes some work, and it seems at times as if few in the Democratic Party even want to try. Most Democrats, including those in the presidential field, engage almost exclusively with tribal liberals and consume only liberal media. They loathe Trump with passion, dismiss and distrust his supporters, and are mostly resistant to his genuine strengths and particular appeal.

To win in 2020, the Democratic hopefuls need to study both Trump and his voters, and they must do it right away. The strategists warn that if the candidates wait until spring or summer, it will be too late. As one puts it, "Don't underestimate Trump, know him."

Starting now, Democratic candidates must be able to conduct their own campaigns for the nomination while simultaneously focusing on how to beat Trump in the general, while always, always assuming he can win.

"You can't just run your own campaign," says Charlie Baker, a veteran of many presidential campaigns, including Hillary Clinton's four years ago. "Everything you do and say publicly has to have a component that speaks to the question of 'what is the right answer about how to deal with Trump?'"

"It's like learning to drive," says another operative. "Learning how to maneuver the car and finding your route is only half the job. You have to be conscious that the driver in the car across the road could barrel into you at any second, and kill you. You have to anticipate the swerves and assume the worst about his character, and find a way to get to your destination safely."

Most Democrats, including Democratic politicians, think Trump's behavior and personality are so blatantly abhorrent that delving more deeply into what makes him tick is foul, irrelevant. But comprehending Trump's motivations and his virtuosity at connecting with voters is crucial to upending his campaign, says John Sasso, the Boston-based longtime strategist. "He may be someone who doesn't look at issues seriously, but he does understand how to communicate in the environment that we are in. And I would never, never, ever take that lightly."

For all the speculation that Trump is unhappy and adrift in Washington, the strategists nevertheless believe he will fight with feral intensity to keep his job. As Baker says, "Nobody lets go of power. It must be taken from them." And Trump knows that he will be viewed as an accident of history if he is denied a second term, a man who lucked into the Oval Office via the machinations of Vladimir Putin, Julian Assange, and James Comey, and failed to be reelected on his own merit. This would make him the lowliest member of the one-term losers club and gives him a strong incentive to scrabble for four more years.

Another incentive, according to Baker, is Trump's fear that, if he does not win, he could go to prison. Baker cites the fate of Trump's former campaign chairman Paul Manafort, currently serving a lengthy prison sentence for bank crimes and fraud. Trump might be thinking, *If it can happen to a guy like Manafort, it can happen to me.* Reelection will buy him four more years, safely ensconced in the Oval Office, to assess his predicament and figure out how to wriggle out of trouble if need be.

It is difficult, say the strategists, to overstate how imposing Trump will be as an adversary. Yet, in their view, many of the Democratic candidates are not taking Trump seriously, dismissing the man as an incompetent clown and his presidency as an unambiguous failure. When your colleagues, friends, and news sources only talk about the Trump administration as a con and a farce, it's hard to imagine voters supporting the president a second time. "I want to give them all a good shake," says one Democratic advisor.

Jennifer Granholm, who was shocked by Hillary Clinton's loss, cautions against Democratic complacency. "I don't think we can underestimate him one jot. I don't believe any of these polls. I think he's extremely dangerous for Democrats. He's going to have a ton of money. He's going to have the Russians and all that. I don't underestimate that. Brad Parscale, his campaign manager, is brilliant in terms of how to use social media to manipulate [voters]."

One person's crook is another person's charmer. Will Robinson ingeniously summarizes Trump's allure. "He's an anti-hero, like Bonnie and Clyde, like Jesse James, like [former Louisiana governor and convicted racketeer] Edwin Edwards, like [former Philadelphia mayor] Frank Rizzo. Frank Rizzo punched a reporter, his favorability went up."

And how does someone achieve that status?

"They become a character, a beloved scoundrel," explains Robinson. "It's like performance art. And a lot of what Trump does is, he's created a movie, *The Trump Movie*. It keeps [his supporters] engaged, it keeps them entertained. And when he does something ridiculous, people say, 'Oh, that's just Trump.'"

It is true that Trump has gotten dozens of free passes simply by being so over-the-top that his bad actions prompt paralyzed astonishment rather than outrage with consequences. "He's [like] the beloved crazy uncle," says Robinson. "He says something ridiculous to you and all the adults roll their eyes, and then he gives you ten bucks. A certain element is a fake authenticity or projecting authenticity. That's what makes him so strong."

A strategist currently working for a presidential campaign says, "[Trump] is shameless. He doesn't worry at all about consistency. He also is able to use his power to communicate to people who also don't like him. He is a narcissist, and because of that he can say things and do things that your typical candidate doesn't say and do, because he actually doesn't have any boundaries in terms of the way he is willing to use the power of the U.S. government. All of those things are huge concerns."

Says Baker, "Trump is clever, not smart. He has the natural instincts of a prizefighter. He has great survival instincts. He will lie about anything. The hardest people to beat are the ones who purposefully act insane."

So everybody agrees: Trump is ruthless and unprincipled and operates by a different set of rules from politicians of the past. But what about all the lies? The literally thousands of blatant, provable, recorded, unambiguous, concrete, irrefutable falsehoods that Trump told while running for president and continues to tell while in office?

Sasso says, "Unfortunately, we are in a time now when the fact-checkers can't possibly catch up with the speed of what's going on and he gets that. He just moves on to the next thing."

Brian Fallon, who was Hillary Clinton's 2016 national press secretary, says, "Most of the voting public thinks that all politicians shade the truth. And so I think that just straight up being a liar, that doesn't work against him. A lot of Democrats might assume that it does at first blush. In fact, I actually think he gets credit for being authentic because the un-PC nature of the things he says in some way work to his advantage with people that might say, 'You know, I don't like that he said that. I thought that was a little bit out of bounds. I wouldn't have said that, but I like the fact that he says what he thinks.' And the impolitic nature of his comments, the often purposely racist or misogynist commentary, are things that cause people to say, 'You know, I like the fact that he's not holding back and he's not trying to please people.'"

Sasso concurs. "[Trump] understands the modern media environment we are in. He is acutely aware of the sense of disrespect many people in the country feel about elites on the coasts. He is unencumbered by truth."

Larry Grisolano, a Chicago strategist who worked on Barack Obama's campaigns, and advises Mayor Pete Buttigieg's 2020 effort, presses this point. "He has a brilliant sense of show craft, of presenting himself and his image [in a way] that projects strength and power. We have a tendency in my party to dismiss that, because it seems so contrived . . . Some of the core things that he has latched onto are very real kind of pressure points in the electorate . . . like trade, immigration, political correctness, the fakery of Washington."

Trump knows how to demonize the privileged and other targeted segments of the electorate to connect with the masses. The phrase *connect with the masses* has an elitist ring, but it describes his reach as well as his fan base, the sheer number of loyalists that must be recognized. His years hosting *The Apprentice* made him a TV star; millions welcomed him into their homes every week and never retracted the invitation. It also characterizes Trump's approach; the accessible appeal of a man who, despite his billions and iconic brand, can craft instant intimacy with ten thousand people in an arena, and multitudes more over the airwaves.

Trump flirted with a presidential bid over the years, teasing and threatening to run for the office, boasting to reporters and the public that he was certain to win if he did, while privately acknowledging the dizzying implausibility of finding success in the unfamiliar arena of politics.

Yet when he finally leaped into the race in 2015, it was no surprise to him that he met a warm reception—not from the press or the Republican Party, but from the citizens who attended his rallies. His events started out large, and became gargantuan. At first, fans who kept dog-eared copies of *The Art of the Deal* on the family bookshelf, or who watched Trump on *The Apprentice* every week, came out to see the famous businessperson. They were accompanied by the curious and the bored. Then the energy changed and the venues expanded. "It's a movement, folks," Trump told his crowds triumphantly, and he was right.

Perhaps Trump had not predicted how smoothly he would ascend to the nomination, nor how swiftly he would dispatch his Republican rivals, but he had been convinced his people would show up in droves to join his movement. Part of his confidence came from a fingertip feel for the populist mood of the country, gleaned from his massive media consumption and his rollicking, bring-the-house-down speeches at events such as the annual Conservative Political Action Conference, or CPAC, a gathering of conservative activists from around the country. But part of his confidence came from the binders.

In the spring of 2011, I was invited to visit Trump Tower and meet with its eponymous owner. The billionaire had spoken at CPAC that February, and I was present to cover the meeting. A number of well-known conservatives and would-be presidential candidates appeared at the event, but when Trump took the stage, the room was packed to the gills with avid listeners, many of them young. The speech Trump gave—vilifying Beltway elites, career politicians, China, Mexico, and illegal immigrants—would become familiar to cable news and YouTube viewers five years later. But in that ballroom on that day, Trump shook the rafters and planted the seeds of his historic White House victory.

It is not difficult to gauge the potency of a political presentation by the intensity of the audience response, but the excitement Trump aroused was exceptional. The CPAC crowd loved Trump's message—not his theatrics or his celebrity, but his message—and the fervent reaction to him far outstripped that of every other speaker, including the many White House hopefuls who sought the GOP nomination in 2012. Soon after Trump's CPAC event, I appeared on television and made those points. I did not in any way endorse Trump's remarks, of course, but merely conveyed the force and power of his display. I said that if Trump chose to enter the Republican presidential nomination fight, his potential should not be underestimated.

Trump was watching the television segment. One sure thing about Donald Trump back then, which is still true to this day: if you said something favorable about him on television, he would call you on the telephone and tell you how smart you are. He phoned me up, thanked me for my comments on his CPAC speech, and invited me to come by Trump Tower and have a little talk about politics. Trump had been a fixture in business, pop culture, the gossip rags, and the modern American psyche since my youth, and for all his cartoonish swank, he was a fascinating figure. Now he was making waves in the world of politics. I accepted.

I arrived at Trump Tower on time, was ushered into his office suite on the twenty-sixth floor, and was told Trump was running behind schedule. Before I settled in to wait, his top in-house political aide scooped me up and led me to his own small office to discuss the viability of a 2012 Trump presidential campaign.

That aide was Michael Cohen, Trump's personal lawyer and fixer, who later became caught up in Robert Mueller's wide-ranging investigation into possible collusion between the Russian government and the 2016 Trump campaign. Cohen publicly broke with his longtime boss, confessed to Mueller, and in December 2018, was sentenced to three years in federal prison after pleading guilty to crimes including campaign finance violations and tax evasion, a "veritable smorgasbord of fraudulent conduct," according to the judge who sentenced him.

At the time of my visit to Trump Tower in 2011, Cohen was the main public face and point of contact for an exploration into a Trump presidential bid, as his boss taped episodes of *The Apprentice*, marketed his brand, dallied with real estate deals, and dipped his toes in and out of the political waters of Iowa, New Hampshire, and beyond. Cohen gabbled about "Mr. Trump" with a breathless reverence that was almost laughable, as if the mogul were some combination of Solomon, Hercules, and Elvis Presley.

I had spoken to Cohen on occasion over the previous few years and was prepared for the song-and-dance boosterism I heard that afternoon. That Mr. Trump was in demand all over the country to give political speeches and share his thoughts on the issues of the day. That Republican Party officials in Iowa and New Hampshire were begging him to run. That the reaction to Mr. Trump's every appearance and event was electric, revolutionary.

Trump and Cohen are very different men, but at the time they were identical in one respect: the ardor with which they could discuss the brains, talents, and general splendor of Donald J. Trump. One tends to absorb such hyperbole with more than a touch of skepticism. I listened with patience and reserve. Then Cohen brought out the binders.

They were filled with letters. Dozens, scores, hundreds of letters. Cohen told me heaps of letters arrived in the mail every day, sent by strangers from all over the country, and that Trump's secretarial team collected, sorted, and organized them into binders. Some were handwritten; some included checks, or five- or ten-dollar bills, or small mementos. All beseeched Trump to run for president.

Cohen flipped through the pages of plastic-encased correspondence, reading aloud from particularly heartwarming, impassioned, or resonant missives. *You HAVE to run . . . America needs you . . . My children's future depends on it . . . The career politicians will never fix our problems*. Cohen's face was alight with devotion, urgency, pride. Idly, I wondered if the letters were genuine. Perhaps they had been generated by a team of underpaid foreign workers; or by the Trump Organization administrative staff; or by Cohen himself, laboring as if over an elementary school art project, with floral stationery, scratch pads, postcards, inkwells, ballpoint pens, and typewriters from eBay set out before him.

But the language in these letters was genuine, the words evocative. Many of the letters echoed the message Trump had delivered at CPAC and other venues. There were citizens all over the country, a significant portion of the electorate, who were struggling, grievously unhappy and afraid. They were in trouble, and they thought America was in trouble too. They had seen this man on television, this man who had so much confidence and so many glib answers, and they wanted him to go to Washington and set things right.

When politicians are deliberating over joining a presidential race, it is common for them to boast that a diverse array of Americans is encouraging them to run. While there is often truth to this claim, the appeals usually come from staff, close friends, and loyal donors who have offered regular support over the years.

Cohen's binders of letters, the outpouring of promises and pleas, were perhaps unprecedented in modern times. The people who wrote to Trump nearly a decade ago would be disappointed when he announced in May 2011 that he would not be entering the 2012 presidential race. "This decision does not come easily or without regret," said Trump in a statement, "especially when my potential candidacy continues to be validated by ranking at the top of the Republican contenders in polls across the country. I maintain the strong conviction that if I were to run, I would be able to win the primary and ultimately, the general election."

Four years later, those binders of letters, I believe, helped inspire Trump to make his victorious bid for the White House. They served as more than an ego stroke, more than the typical fan blandishments dashed off to a reality TV star. They were a tangible sign that the people were waiting for him. Despite the media mockery, despite the dubious mutterings and nervous sneers from the Republican Party, the letters in those binders were the start of something bigger than a campaign. They were the start of a movement.

• • •

"I don't think we can underestimate Trump's power," says Jim Margolis, a veteran of the Kerry, Obama, and Hillary Clinton campaigns, who now advises Senator Kamala Harris. "He won 63 million votes. He essentially owns his own network, Fox News, that he uses as his personal communications outlet. He has 45 million Twitter followers. Millions of Facebook followers. He has a large megaphone and an ability to excite his base. His people will turn out no matter what he does. Trump is formidable, and dismissing him would be a huge mistake."

Trump understands exactly how to maneuver these assets. Mike McCurry, a longtime Democratic spokesman who served in that role in Bill Clinton's White House, describes Trump's strength as coming "from his knowledge of what moves mass audiences, which comes from his experience on television. Not many elite, overachieving, Ivy League–educated politicians have that. Trump knows what Americans are interested in."

Says Robinson, "I think that he's a master of narrative. Stories, stories, stories. Democrats are stuck in their frontal lobes, you know, we're stuck on math and issues and that sort of thing. The reality is a story will beat a sack full of facts any day."

Winter came for Westeros, and now it is coming for the U.S. "Did you watch *Game of Thrones*?" Robinson asks. "In the end, when they try to select a king, one of the characters says, 'In order to select the best king, we need to select the person with the best story.' We are writing a bunch of position papers, while he's writing a narrative."

In a way, Trump created an entirely new model for running for president—replacing experience and gravitas with aggression and chutzpah—and everyone else is going to have to transform or perish.

"In 2016, he changed the rules," states Donna Brazile, the former campaign manager for Al Gore and past interim chair of the Democratic National Committee. "He changed the rules on how to run for president. And he changed the rules on how presidential candidates are perceived by the public."

Brazile believes Trump has altered what many Americans expect a president to achieve. "He's a cultural champion. He's a legend among voters who believe that because Washington is in his way, he can't get the job done. There's a Trump phenomenon." And that makes him ever more daunting as an opponent. "The guy has a gift," Brazile says. "I don't know if he got it from real estate or from being on reality TV. Whatever it is, defeating Donald Trump is not going to be as easy as people think. It requires a lot of work."

Says Grisolano, "There is this idea that politics is disingenuous and that people have this politeness about their opponents, even though everybody knows they hate their guts, and that there's this kind of disingenuous show in Washington. I think he peeled back the veil on that in a way that people identify with. And that really kind of finds a pressure point relative to what's wrong with Washington, what's wrong with politics. Like everything else, when you take it to the extreme, and he ends up in the territory of hate speech and white nationalism, then I think he's sort of reached negative returns. But at the core of this idea of being too polite all the time when it's disingenuous, I think it's something that people relate to."

Mainstream media outlets have wondered in stark print if Trump is actually a sociopath (his narcissism seems fairly irresistible for most to diagnose), and there is a view that Trump is so transparently selfish and soulless that his supporters themselves must be morally challenged. But John Sasso disputes this motif. Know Trump, he says, but know his voter too.

"I think people misunderstand what's going on here," Sasso says. "This narrative that people think he's a liar and he's a crook and he has no character, but they're willing to support him anyway. I think his people think he has character. They define character differently than many voters, but they believe he has character. And what they say about that is, 'He's keeping his word. He promised he'd take on Washington, he promised to take on immigrants.' You promise this, promise that. He seems to be doing that. That's character to them. Never mind that he is not telling the truth. And that he just says whatever he needs to say to get by the next ten minutes, which is what he deals with. It doesn't matter that an hour later he'll change his mind. They view that as character in a certain way."

Most citizens, including some of the president's fans, do not bother to dissect every Trump statement or misstatement, or mock every oddball tweet or covfefe. They do not have the time or inclination to devote such energy to the day-to-days of the political game.

"What makes him formidable," says a strategist who has worked on presidential campaigns back to the 1980s, "is that he lies and he leaves the impression still with too many people that he is a president for them. People don't watch TV, or pay attention to Twitter, or watch cable networks the way we do, and they just don't know. I go to Michigan; it's a different world there. It's something that they know about but not like we do, so they only hear things in different pieces. When CNN or MSNBC are trying to say it's his 10,964th lie, people back in Ohio and Michigan don't hear that. They just don't. I think many people still think he is the person who is going to make their lives better."

And when they do pay attention, they hear Trump speaking in a language that is comfortable and relatable. "The guy understands how to communicate," says Sasso, who thinks Democrats are completely ignoring this lesson. "His clarity, his sense of repetition. The man is not a buffoon." Sasso notes that Trump rarely uses political jargon, in style or content. Very few voters want to hear politicians speak like politicians. Such rhetoric can be patronizing as well as dull.

McCurry tells of working for the 1984 presidential campaign of Ohio senator John Glenn, the former astronaut portrayed by Ed Harris in the hit film *The Right Stuff*, which premiered one year before the election in October 1983. Starstruck voters came out to see Glenn and were more often than not disappointed when he talked like a politician, rather than an astronaut. Glenn's run for the White House fell back to Earth, fast.

Trump, meanwhile, speaks simply, without pretension, sometimes off-the-cuff. His vocabulary is limited, which can be rendered as crude, yet his speeches are easy to listen to, entertaining, yet not without a sort of emotive substance. He knows how to use common language to form a bond with his audience, which he then leverages to arouse anger, inspire passion, and cement loyalty. "He's created an identity for people," says pollster Mark Mellman. "He's defined who the 'us' is and who the 'them' is, and he uses that emotional dynamic to elevate his support."

Trump has been particularly effective at reaching white working-class voters, a group that has felt under economic and cultural siege over the last several generations. Strategists in both parties note that Trump did not create the Trump coalition; he simply saw it, took ownership of it, and stoked it. Its origins go back decades, to the 1970s, when the promise of the American Dream began to fade and people stopped believing their children would have the same economic opportunities as they did growing up. They became increasingly distrustful of most large institutions, especially the federal government. Trump's maverick persona, his status as a true outsider but a bona fide celebrity and a bully with brio, matched up cleanly with their weary desire for a universal reckoning. They felt Trump was giving them back their pride.

And Trump has not just won their devotion, but has united them against a range of common enemies. To be sure, Trump has employed unsavory rhetoric and methods—racial dog whistles, shameless bluster, cruel abuse of his enemies, assaults on basic American freedoms. But, the strategists say, Trump has instinctively seized upon the issues that rouse political passion—immigration, China, trade, late-term abortion—whether he personally cares about them or not.

And Bill Carrick, who worked on presidential campaigns for Ted Kennedy and Dick Gephardt, adds that Democrats need to understand that Trump does not pay a price for attacking the sanctity of America's great institutions. Outside of elites, most voters, even those on the left, are not big defenders of the judiciary, the Fed, Congress, or the media—all frequent Trump objects of ridicule. These elite institutions are not unpopular because the president has attacked them; he attacks them because he knows that voters view them with disdain and distrust.

The vague issue platform Trump offered as a candidate in 2016 and the policies he has pursued as president matter far less to this group, Mellman says, than Trump's ability to offer them an identity, a sense of pride. The Democratic nominee needs to understand how Trump pulled off this feat and re-create her or his own version of the very same thing. Democrats, including Hillary Clinton, have had a hard time executing this strategy. There is nothing more difficult for a politician than generating genuine passion. Voters are disillusioned with Washington, the pettiness, the dysfunction, the decaying political parties. They have busy lives and real problems. For the president's contingent of blue-collar white Americans, Trump provided an outlet for their resentments and promised to make things better.

Take China, for example. For years, leading Democrats, from Speaker Nancy Pelosi to Senator Charles Schumer to Hillary Clinton, have warned about China as an economic and military threat to the United States. But their public presentations about the problem have tended toward policy prescriptions, rather than the kind of emotional, story-based communication Trump utilizes. Trump talks in a conversational, confidential manner about China, braising his remarks with his facile businessman's experiences. He invites members of his base to participate in an urgent, global crusade to retrieve American dough and dignity from a ruthless foreign power, investing them further in his policy plans.

Far too many Democratic leaders and candidates dismiss Trump's core followers as ignorant plebeians. But Trump's fans are American citizens. They work. They raise families. They spend time with friends. They pay taxes. They vote.

It is vital, says Sasso, that the Democratic candidates immediately "separate [their] own feelings about Trump and his supporters from how you deal with them. You need to treat them with respect. When you deal with Trump supporters, you can't take the Hillary approach that they're unethical, or the Obama notion that they only care about their guns. You need to talk to these people in a straightforward way, understanding that they have grievances, they have concerns. There's a portion of them, not all of them, but there's a substantial portion that you need to treat with respect, not for their belief in Trump himself or what he stands for, but you have to respect them and you have to have a dialogue with them. I think the people that say, 'I won't go on Fox News,' I think they're making a mistake. I think you have to be willing to address Trump supporters in a way that shows a certain respect towards them as individuals."

Warns Jeff Link, an experienced operative based in Iowa, "The Democrats have to stop condescending to rural voters. We fell into that trap in the past, and we will never have a shot at winning back rural voters until we stop condescending. You can't say, 'If you voted for Trump then you are racist, misogynist, or stupid.' Trump's appeal is cultural. If you look at his policies, they are devastating to rural America. But they are voting culturally, because he said to them, 'Your way of life should be celebrated.' Democrats said, 'You've either got to move to the cities or you've got to change.'"

Of all the unforced errors Hillary Clinton made in her loss to Donald Trump, referring to his backers as "a basket of deplorables" and "irredeemable" was probably the most arrant.

"I kept saying in 2016, 'I don't want to call these people names,'" says Brazile. "'I don't want to give them some kind of distinction without honor.' I was there when Hillary used the word 'deplorables.' I want to make sure that we are able to connect to these voters because they put Obama in the White House. I mean how do you go back and say 'they're racist,' when they actually voted for Obama?" Brazile is sympathetic to the nuances. "They felt they were left on the outskirts of hope and not given a chance to come back into the circle of opportunity. And they believed that Donald Trump could deliver for them."

One strategist who worked on Hillary Clinton's campaign deeply regrets the way the team addressed these voters. "If I have a criticism of the '16 race, it was that we did not see them."

McCurry agrees that the candidates must "avoid the arrogance of 'I'm smarter than you are, I know more than you do.' We live in different camps. It reflects the polarization that is obvious in our political culture now. You've got to attract some of those Trump voters . . . You don't speak their language, you don't have the vocabulary that reaches the people that Trump manages to reach. You are speaking at a different level and you are not boiling things down to some basics that people will grab ahold of and say, 'That makes senses to me.'"

This does not, of course, mean that some of Trump's voters are not in fact racists. And how exactly does a Democratic leader handle American citizens who are racist and bigoted? It is a line candidates must tread with great care and concern, for reasons of morality, history, personal integrity, and the reputation of the United States as an entity. Far too often when issues of racism arise, Trump plays both sides, feigning mild perturbation when performing for the mainstream media and citizenry, while sending signals to segregationists and bigots that he is on their side. He would rather have the vote of a racist than no vote at all.

This is why Trump refused to renounce his role as a leader of the Birther movement, the racist conspiracy theory that posited Obama was born in Kenya rather than Hawaii. It is why he was at times reluctant to reject the endorsement of David Duke, the former Grand Wizard of the Ku Klux Klan. It is why, when a young woman was killed and several dozen more injured while peacefully protesting a rally of white supremacists in Charlottesville, Virginia, in August 2017, Trump responded with careful neutrality. "We condemn in the strongest possible terms this egregious display of hatred, bigotry, and violence on many sides, on many sides," he said. Trump did not enjoy the controversy, but nor did he have the slightest interest in alienating some of the most stalwart and reliable factions of his base. His reaction to Charlottesville was one of the bleakest and most shameful moments of his presidency. It is why he singled out four Democratic House members, female women of color who were challenging his agenda, and told them to leave the United States. "Why don't they go back and help fix the totally broken and crime-infested places from which they came," the president tweeted, ignoring the fact that three of the four women were born in the United States. "Then come back and show us how it is done. These places need your help badly, you can't leave fast enough. I'm sure that Nancy Pelosi would be very happy to quickly work out free travel arrangements!"

Navigating how to talk about race under the broader circumstances of American life is complicated, the strategists acknowledge. When nearly the entire Republican Party, including its elected officials, backs Trump, and is thus complicit in his racial and sometimes racist appeals, it requires a deft touch to speak to Trump supporters with a directness that is not offensive to them, and does not trouble or depress the Democratic base.

Says one strategist with long-standing ties to the Clintons, "He very well might win again. Everybody who is not doing well [economically] feels that it's because other people got in line [ahead of them]. And that is just not true. He just plays on everyone's fears and insecurities. It's just race-baiting. It's just crazy. It's like watching an old television movie, where things that wouldn't be in the movie anymore are back in the movie. It is so unreal. We just went retro."

Says Pete Giangreco, another Obama campaign aide, who has advised Amy Klobuchar's 2020 campaign, "Some of [Trump's voters] were voting to validate the racism. That's why this guy never stops talking about things like immigration, NFL football players taking a knee, and why white cops are good and why criminals are bad. He's constantly mining that fault line, trying to dig it deeper or trying to push it wider. And those people are probably off-limits to us. Some of them are Democrats, some of them are union members. The people that are motivated against political correctness, we're never going to get those folks back. Some are Democrats and some are independents. A lot of them are Republicans. The whole Charlottesville thing and everything else, it just sort of validates the fact that for those people who do think things were better in the '50s, we're never going to get those folks because I think they're voting culturally, they're not voting for change or strength or economics."

That is the key: Democratic candidates have to appeal to Trump's voters in the same way he does, without debasing their own integrity. Some strategists say the way to find this balance is to keep a close hold on optimism, clarity, humanity, and mutual respect while selling their message to all Americans.

How do you change people's minds without stealing their pride?

"You need to be able to tell a better story about America than he does," says one top Hillary Clinton aide from 2016. "And [Trump] has a pretty compelling, a very dark and compelling story that he tells about America that many people thought made a lot of sense. He makes their lives make sense. They are proud to be American again. He validates their world-view, and that is very important to them. These voters have a high pain threshold. You see people hurt by his tariffs and they don't care. They say, 'Look, we didn't get into this problem over-night. It's going to take a long time for Trump to turn the ship around. It's hard to manage in the short term, but eventually we will get to a place where China is not kicking our ass every day.'

"So I think that this notion that Trump voters are stupid because 'he's not helping you, you haven't gotten anything out of his tax plan' [isn't fruitful]," she adds. "They don't care. A lot of them don't care. They think that he is putting the country on the right path. And that's very valuable to them. You have to tell a better story about America than he does. You have to make those people feel like they're part of America. Like everyone has got a place here. Everyone has got a future here. Democrats have a hurdle to overcome to not be seen as judging people. Respect the lives that they lead and the work that they do. That is the thing that's in your control to be able to combat Trump."

The Democrats must accept that many millions of people who voted for Trump are not racist. Or ignorant, or stupid, or hate-filled, or mean-spirited, or uneducated. Some of them never much cared for Trump but thought him the better choice.

"I think that most Democrats fundamentally misunder-stand where the electorate that we most need to win is when it comes to this guy," says a strategist now working for a Demo-cratic challenger. "Many of them voted for him even though they did not like him. Many of the people who voted for him who do not like him still do not like him. They give him a kind of grudging respect for having done what he said he would do."

This set of voters will not necessarily fall over laughing every time Trump makes a vulgar crack. They may not respect his obeisance to dictators such as Putin and Kim Jong-un. They may weep when they see images of children suffering in detention centers on the Mexican border. But they also may approve of a more conservative judiciary and tougher stances on immigration and trade. They may be grateful for a more vibrant economy and a Beltway reckoning. On balance, they may not necessarily be unhappy with the direction of the country or the policy results of the Trump administration. They may not be so vitally impatient for another change in 2020. Their votes may be gettable, but what will the Democrats offer them?

The first thing candidates can give these people is attention.

"If you want to win the general election," says a strategist not affiliated with a candidate, "you have to have regular, daily contact with these people, these Trump supporters. You've got to make a connection, and get them to really hear you. You have to find a way to reach them every day if you can, so they know you as well as you know them. They will listen to good ideas. If you offer a better option than what Trump has to offer, they'll vote for you."

McCurry and others reiterate this point. Candidates should meet with persuadable Trump voters as soon as possible and talk with them in a low-key setting, without the media around to interpret or judge or distract. "Make time in your schedule right now, before spring, before the nomination, to listen to their voices," says a strategist. "Use that precious time. Hear their concerns, seek them out. Especially ones who voted once or twice for Obama."

Then the candidates can work their stories into stump speeches, understand a variety of the electorate's fears and dreams, and begin to alter the way they speak, so their general election vocabulary does not seem phony or political.

One strategist suggests it would be smart for a candidate to do one of the campaign's closing events before the Iowa caucuses in Howard County, which is north of Waterloo and east of Mason City, near the Minnesota border. That county flipped a remarkable 42 percentage points from Obama's victory over Romney in 2012 to a Trump landslide just four years later.

Do not be indignant, say the strategists. Do not be intimidated. Just listen and learn. The Democratic candidates will have to be open to new rules and fresh ideas and a shifting constituency, and like Trump, embrace the sensibilities of the country, no matter how unorthodox and cosmetic they may appear.

As Will Robinson says, Democrats need to capture the public imagination the way Trump can, and he offers a classic example.

After months of working with the current administration to advance criminal justice reform, reality star Kim Kardashian West joined Trump in the East Room of the White House on June 13, 2019, to promote a measure to facilitate prisoner reentry. Kardashian West offered her warm gratitude for Trump's actions, saying, "I just want to thank the president for really standing behind this issue. And seeing the compassion that he's had for criminal justice has been really remarkable." Trump praised her in turn. "I guess she's pretty popular," he said.

Robinson marvels at this coup. "His whole criminal justice reform, right, who'd he do it with? A Kardashian? That's like popular culture royalty. And it's brilliant. That's just brilliant."

CHAPTER TWO

BATTLE TESTING

LESSON: GET READY
TO GO AGAINST TRUMP.

So now we know how Candidate Trump goes about securing votes. We know his skill sets and audacity are unique in modern politics. And we know, for his challengers, there is no time to waste. How can the Democrats sidestep Trump's game, even the playing field—and win this time?

According to John Sasso, serious candidates are expected to present a positive message, especially on the economy; a negative message, or "frame," for the opposition; and an attractive persona with clear-cut traits, ideally those of strength, conviction, and empathy. Sasso says it is important that the message as a whole reflects the authentic core of each candidate—voters instinctively identify and ultimately reject artifice and blandishments.

All the strategists agree that each 2020 Democratic candidate should immediately settle on a campaign philosophy, begin to present his or her policy arguments, and court a sincere, long-term relationship with the voters.

The checklist?

Schedule major speeches, give intimate talks, charm at house parties, sit for national and local interviews, and erect a solid online presence. The press will get sick of hearing the same message repeated over and over, but the public only tunes in sporadically, some early and some late. For a candidate, there is no such thing as too soon, especially when crafting and honing an effective argument. And when facing an opponent as imposing as Trump, the Democrats will need as much practice as possible.

For all of Trump's inconsistencies and thrashing about, one of his advantages, say the strategists, is the stability of his brand as the cocky, business-savvy, anti-establishment anti-hero. Trump shows up in character every day. If a Democratic candidate cannot forge her or his own narrative, and consistently reinforce it with a confident policy agenda, an appealing nature, and a clear argument against four more years of Donald Trump, then the winter primary season will be cold and short.

The strategists believe that the environment in which Donald Trump got elected is still very much in place. Despite a somewhat improved economy, voters also feel the volatility. Americans remain insecure, unhappy with Washington and career politicians, and looking for a change. Historically, the more optimistic candidate tends to win U.S. general elections. But Trump's 2016 victory demonstrated that a large segment of voters wants an oddball cocktail of anger as well as optimism.

Democrats should be cautioned that the war against the elites is not over. "The Democratic nominee," says Charlie Baker, "cannot go back to a pre-Brexit world."

In other words, the candidates must temper an optimistic theme with an acknowledgment of the negative feelings coursing through the electorate. If they start with a generic positive message that does not tell a story and ignores the voters' daily reality, many will tune them out.

Candidates should give themselves room to react to events of the day in an instinctive, natural way. It is appropriate for candidates to show anger or sadness or irritation when they are genuinely angry or sad or irritated. Authentic responses can reflect the public mood and give them credibility with voters when they present their solutions.

As a number of the strategists point out, one of Trump's great strengths is something the media often cast as a weakness. An event occurs, in Washington, in Hollywood, somewhere else in the U.S., somewhere in the world, and Trump gets reflexively and viscerally ticked off about it. And he often takes his grievance to Twitter, which suggests to real people that his reply is genuine and unmediated by political advisors. A Twitter-happy finger might be unpresidential, but it is accessibly human. It comes off as authentic, it garners oversized attention, and it allows the president to dominate the news cycle. Controlling the news cycle is half the battle in a presidential campaign.

Trump was an expert at monopolizing news cycles even before he ran for president, and the capability to change the story of the day at will is one of the top assets for any incumbent. The president of the United States can always find a way to summon the eyes of the world at a moment's notice. With Trump in office, his capacity to set the agenda is exponentially multiplied. The Democratic challengers should accept right now that, over the course of the next year, this dynamic will always be present.

Says one member of Hillary Clinton's 2016 team, "You're not going to out-news the guy. You're not going to defeat him in dominating news coverage. You're not going to be able to do that. The Democratic nominee is not going to be able to do that. Everybody says, 'You've got to create your own weather and you've got to create your news, and you can't let him dominate the news coverage.' And it's not in your power to do that if you're not willing to be as outrageous as him, and the Democrat is not going to be as willing to be as outrageous as he is."

Heeding this key point could save the Democrats untold time and frustration. It would be futile, she says, to try to beat Trump at his favorite game. The candidate would get dirty, and the president would almost certainly come out on top, anyway. But "there are things you can do with different digital tools to communicate with people where they are, and that can be helpful," she says. "He is always going to dominate at the top layer of coverage. Just because he is dominating the news doesn't mean that it can't accrue to your candidate's benefit, particularly if he is being outrageous."

Brian Fallon notes that Democrats are not inclined to throw Trump-sized tantrums in any case. "I think what [Trump] does that a generic Democrat is not wired to do," says Fallon, "is he identifies issues that he wants to brand himself with and courts controversy on purpose in order to enliven a stance that he wants to have penetrate. And people get distracted by the controversial nature of the stance he's taking. It's not in the DNA of most Democrats to stake out a position on a 52- to 48-percent issue, let alone on an idea that is [unpopular]."

Fallon recalls that four years ago, Trump guaranteed himself extra attention from voters and the press by deliberately approaching issues from controversial angles. As Fallon puts it, Trump calculated that "I want to be seen as the top person on border security. So let me go and just openly express racist thoughts on Mexicans. I want to be seen as the toughest guy on national security or terror, so I will propose a ban on all Muslim immigration."

A little emotion goes a long way. Will Robinson thinks that Democratic bigwigs spent too much time in high school debate clubs, coolly and methodically marshaling facts to win arguments. The Democratic Party, he says, would be better off if it drew its leadership from theater majors who know how to tap into their emotions and tell a good story.

The Democratic candidates need to show emotion when critiquing the status quo, says Jennifer Granholm. This might be a particular challenge for the female candidates, she acknowledges, because many members of the media and some voters react differently when women politicians display passion.

As Larry Grisolano observes, "We are still in an era of change. People are not satisfied with Washington." Trump, he says, was effective running as an outsider in 2016, and has successfully positioned himself, despite being an incumbent president, as the candidate of change for 2020. The strategists say that the Democratic candidates have to redefine what change means, demonstrate that they are capable of following through on promises, and make clear that they, too, are troubled by the past and understand people are frightened for the future.

"These candidates really have to show some fire in the belly and passion to match Trump," says one operative. "One of the things Trump does really well is he shows passion. I don't know if it's made up or not, I don't really care, but he shows passion. They have to roll up their sleeves and show the passion they have for why someone should vote for them."

. . .

Once the candidates have connected with voters in a human way, they will have to come up with an actual policy plan to prove they can do the job. That still matters, even in the era of Trump. And they need to know how to market their platform.

Craig Smith, who worked on the presidential campaigns of Bill Clinton and Al Gore, says, "There's a large group of people in this country that when they look at the future, they see it coming at them like a freight train, and they don't see how they fit in it. We have to have a message for those people and explain to them how they fit in the country that we're going to be ten years from now. Donald Trump said, 'You know what, I'm going to make you fit by taking us back to the 1960s.' Okay, you can't go back. But we didn't explain to them how they fit in the 2020s, and we have to have a plan for that. That is the most important thing I think we can do. And it's got to be simple and it's got to be explainable and has got to be sincere. You can't treat rural or non-college people like they are problems to be solved. They're all Americans too. We're all in this together, and you have got to convey that to them. 'You're part of this country, too, and here is what we're going to do for you.' I just think that wasn't done well in 2016."

"You can't just run a campaign saying 'Trump is a bum,'" says Bob Shrum, a fixture in many Democratic presidential campaigns for decades. "You have to have a vision for the economy. Hillary's slogan was a critique of Trump, not her own message."

The history of American presidential campaigns is cluttered with slogans. Some are vague (*Facing the Future*, William Jennings Bryan, 1908), some specific (*Tippecanoe and Tyler Too*, William Henry Harrison, 1840), some practical (*Don't Swap Horses When Crossing Streams*, Abraham Lincoln, 1864), some bald (*Vote as You Shot*, Ulysses S. Grant, 1868). They can rhyme (*All the Way with LBJ*, Lyndon B. Johnson, 1964), be declarative (*A Chicken in Every Pot and a Car in Every Garage*, Herbert Hoover, 1928), be defiant (*From Atlanta Prison to the White House*, Eugene V. Debs, 1920), or be melodic (*Happy Days Are Here Again*, Franklin D. Roosevelt, 1932). Some are memorable (*I Like Ike*, Dwight D. Eisenhower, 1952), some forgettable (*We're on Your Side*, Michael Dukakis, 1988), some good (*A Kinder, Gentler Nation*, George H. W. Bush, 1988), some bad (*Jeb!* Jeb Bush, 2016).

The very best slogans, even if unofficial, spring organically from a candidate's persona and public image, from the bond formed with the voters. *Are You Better Off Than You Were Four Years Ago?* Ronald Reagan asked in 1980. Y*es We Can*, Obama promised purringly in 2008. Great slogans capture the ethos of the campaign, present the soul and spirit of the candidate, and stick in the minds of the voters all the way through Election Day and into history.

In 2016, Hillary Clinton picked her slogan, *Stronger Together*, off a list of eighty-five options compiled by a committee of consultants assigned to the task. The phrase was so dry, so meaningless, so hollow that even her own advisors often had trouble summoning it to mind. Trump, on the other hand, chose a slogan that launched a million hats: *Make America Great Again*. That phrase has become one of the most divisive and inflammatory in American political history, but it was catchy, memorable, evocative, and emblematic of Trump's message.

The *Stronger Together* slogan received a soft launch in May 2016, as Clinton slipped it into interviews and campaign trail rhetoric, and then was sent out into the marketplace in the summer, where it was met with shrugs. After Clinton added Virginia senator Tim Kaine as her running mate, she insisted, against the advice of many around her, on putting out a quickie campaign book using *Stronger Together* as the title. The book was a collection of policy proposals and political pabulum.

Clinton was warned that such a book would likely garner weak sales, but she was adamant it be produced. She recounted the great success her husband and Al Gore had in 1992 with their slogan-titled campaign-year book, *Putting People First*. That tome, featuring the handsome visages of the two strapping baby boomers, became an instant *New York Times* bestseller when it was published in September 1992, two months before Election Day.

Bill and Al had a book. Tim and I should have one, too, Hillary told her team.

The book *Stronger Together*, printed with a cover photo of Hillary and Kaine, side by side, smiling and waving gaily, sold fewer than three thousand copies its first week of release, then dropped like a stone, a complete flop, despite being hawked at Democratic rallies and events around the country.

Make America Great Again was not an original sentiment, but it captured the imaginations of Republican voters and became ubiquitous across the nation, a symbol of Trump's message, vogue, and political might. It is likely that, in the fall of 2016, the majority of people in North America (and, perhaps, Europe and Asia) could automatically reel off the MAGA slogan. But if in that same period you were to ask virtually anyone on the streets of Brooklyn, where the Clinton headquarters was located, to recite her slogan, the response would have been a blank stare.

Trump has said that his slogans for the 2020 race will be *Keep America Great* and *Promises Made, Promises Kept*, or a continuation of *Make America Great Again*. The strategists stress that his 2020 Democratic opponent must take the time to come up with a strong slogan to accompany a strong message. "It might be hard to compete with MAGA," says one strategist, "but please put in some time and really think it through. It wouldn't hurt to do a little soul searching. The slogan should actually mean something, even if Trump's is bullshit."

Doug Sosnik, one of Bill Clinton's top political advisors in the White House, says that the eventual nominee cannot assume that Trump will be automatically disqualified because his presidency so often seems in disarray, nothing more than a series of MAGA-infused rallies and pronouncements. Uncommitted voters will not trade in the duffer they have got without a sense of what they will be getting instead. The strategists all promise that a Democrat can appeal to both the base and persuadable voters by offering a solid and specific vision for the economy and other fertile policy areas such as health care, education, and housing, as long as it is presented with verve and style. "You have to create a story every day that reflects your fundamental message," advises Shrum.

Says the former Kansas governor Kathleen Sebelius, "I'm a believer that campaigns are about hearts and minds, and if our campaign is just about minds, we lose. We have to have a nominee who actually is inspirational and aspirational, who really does have an ability to mobilize folks and make people feel that there is hope about the future. It is very critical to have a candidate who can frame a message and tell a story. It has to be a lot more about the future than the past. What electing that candidate will do to improve, change, and stabilize the lives of the people, particularly those who feel overlooked and neglected. They want their lives and their kids' lives and their grandkids' lives to improve, to feel a sense that there is some hopefulness, not that we are on the brink of disaster. Our candidate has to bring a mission of joyfulness and optimism about the future with some very specific plans."

And then it is on the candidate to take down Trump. The media will not do it, warns Jill Alper, even though the press will be rife with stories about the president's immorality and ineptitude. But there is no substitute for the Democratic nominee making the case directly, Alper says, and the argument has got to be tight, unassailable.

An aide to a leading Democratic candidate notes that, in 2016, the Clinton campaign tried to convince voters that Trump was not a successful businessperson. It proved hard to do because *The Apprentice* had already established that aspect of his brand. "People felt like they knew Trump already in 2016," the strategist says. "[Voters would say] 'You are telling me he is not a good businessman? That is the one thing I know about him.'"

So how should a Democratic candidate shape the attack? Get inside Trump's head, says Tad Devine, who has worked on many presidential efforts, most recently for Bernie Sanders in 2016. Other strategists concur. The trick is to launch substantive critiques on policy in areas that hit Trump's ego as well. Turn his perceived assets into deficiencies, his professed toughness into recklessness. "Take what people think is a strength, as [Bush] did with [John] Kerry as a war veteran [in 2004] and flip it," says John Sasso. "You have to show what looks like strength is really weakness, insecurity. When you pick on people that are weak and vulnerable, that is a weakness."

Bill Carrick says the candidates should go straight for Trump's record on the economy. Highlight his weak trade plans, risky tariff proposals, irresponsibility regarding the Fed, and growing budget deficits. Demonstrate that Trump is in over his head.

Adds Governor Sebelius, "Reminding people what a president can and should be doing and what this president hasn't and isn't capable of doing is really important."

Pete Giangreco also says that the economy will be Trump's weakest spot, both substantively and personally. "I think most people believe the economy is stable, is good, is chugging along, but a lot of people who are up for grabs in this election feel like the economy is working for somebody, but not working for them." Trump has personally profited from some of his own policies, Giangreco says, which is a bad look for a president who got elected in part because he promised to improve the lives of poor and middle-class voters. "If you can show that [he's taken advantage], many of those people will turn on him. His supporters really do believe he's defending them. We need to show that his positions on taxes or whatever it is really are against the interests of the average working person that he says he's representing—against their interest in a specific way, and yet to his benefit. He's gotten campaign contributions. He's gotten special deals for coal companies. I think that is an important element of turning people against him and at the same time reminding those that are inclined to be against him, why he is such a despicable, dishonorable individual and terrible example for the country—that he is all self-serving."

Robinson agrees. Transform Trump from a beguiling anti-hero into an out-and-out villain. "How do you beat Jesse James? [You make it clear to voters that] Jesse James just robbed *your* bank and took *your* money."

The "who is on your side" argument is one of the most important in any presidential election, and Granholm believes this is one of the principal explanations for how Trump was able to win in 2016. "I so strongly believe that the answer is that when he said 'the forgotten American,' those to me were the most key words that he used that resonated with people who feel like 'politicians are corrupt, they have left me behind. They're not seeing me.' The candidate who demonstrates they can see people who don't have fat wallets, are not in the cities, who are not part of a traditional cluster of voters [will prevail] . . . Demonstrating that the Democrats have not lost their way and are not hostage to investment bankers in D.C. or wine sippers in San Francisco, that is critical for whoever is the nominee."

The strategists suggest finding some real voters with real stories to tell about their experiences under the Trump administration. "Trump's policies have actually hurt a lot of people," observes one presidential campaign veteran. "The Democratic nominee can get a lot of mileage out of finding a few of these people and letting them make the argument from a heartfelt, individual, totally sympathetic perspective."

Trump is adept at weaving the experiences of regular citizens into the narrative of his core message. Often, these stories are grim and provocative; during the 2016 campaign, he regularly referred by name to Americans murdered by illegal immigrants from Mexico. But he also invited men and women with inspirational stories to his State of the Union addresses, and cheered on American heroes at his controversial 2019 Independence Day event. The Democrats, the strategists insist, should find their own cast of characters, people who once believed in Trump and have suffered for it. "Get these people out front," says a Democratic advisor. "Put them out there in the conversation with social media and advertising, have them appear at rallies. Hillary did this a little with the Gold Star family of [the late United States Army officer Humayun] Khan, but we need to do more this time. And there are a lot of compelling characters with compelling stories. We just have to find them."

The process of corralling these individuals should begin in winter, the earlier the better, even considering the limited time and resources of primary campaigns. Involving genuine American citizens is always considered beneficial in a campaign, but in the chaos of the general election, it is difficult to locate, thoroughly vet, and schedule compelling, reliable individuals. As Sasso says, "If you can get a coal miner, if you can get a local official who supported [the president], to say, 'I supported Donald Trump, but when I realized that what he was doing was hurting me and helping him, that's turned me against him forever.' I would urge people to look at that. I think that could be incredibly effective if you can get the right people who are credible."

The candidates themselves also have to be able to speak convincingly about real problems. Granholm, who served as Michigan's governor from 2003 to 2011, says that "Trump's magic in Michigan was that he came and talked about NAFTA in such a compelling way. [We need] somebody who comes and says, 'I get why people see these hulking shells of factories as empty tributes to NAFTA, sitting on Main Streets in towns all over the Midwest, as testimony to the unfettered trade policies that have not worked for everyday people. I get it. And we're not going to allow that to happen.'"

Jill Alper, too, cites Trump's adroit campaign approach in Michigan, a make-or-break state for the Democrats. "You have to show that you get it. So when you're in Michigan, the first words out of your mouth need to be 'this is a sham' or 'this is ridiculous.' Or 'this is wrong, we're working too hard.'" Many believe that Hillary Clinton was unable to win the "who is on your side" argument in 2016 because of some of the life choices she made after her 2008 presidential run, including the lucrative paid speeches she gave to Wall Street firms. Trump, a billionaire, was able to further cast Clinton as greedy and out-of-touch because he understood why the speeches made voters so angry. He was able to access that anger empathetically, while Clinton's response was remote, defensive, and squirrelly.

A minority of the strategists, however, believe the Democrats should use a different frame against the incumbent, one very similar to Clinton's blueprint in 2016.

Barack Obama's chief strategist, David Axelrod, says, "The most compelling, broad-based argument is to run against the sheer sense of exhaustion that Trump has created, the daily barrage of tweets and tantrums: the nasty, gratuitous fights and unremitting divisiveness; the constant sense of chaos that stands in the way of progress. We know it will not change. Can America stand four more years of that?"

Both arguments—a critique of the Trump economy and an indictment of Trump's values, morality, and style—will inevitably be part of the Democratic nominee's message. Making the decision about which one to emphasize is among the top priorities for all the candidates in the winter.

•   •   •

As Clinton learned, Trump's unorthodox and unabashed tactics create asymmetrical warfare, and his methodology presents a variety of challenges that often dovetail and fuse. When Jeb Bush was running against Trump for the nomination in 2016, he aptly called him "a chaos candidate." Trump regularly lobs controversial statements that seem to serve no purpose other than to provoke the left, or even the right (such as expressing support for gay rights and Planned Parenthood), and ultimately confuse and discombobulate everybody. Brian Fallon calls these throwaways "random banana peels," and they prove again and again that Trump inexplicably plays by different rules without paying a price.

Sebelius warns, "He clearly doesn't care if what he says is accurate and can be disproven immediately. As long as he says it and says it all often enough, it becomes sort of a factoid. So it's a very different kind of campaign than most people have ever seen. And so I think any candidate who goes in thinking 'this is the classic run against this guy, say all the bad things about him and then you will do just fine,' is just dead wrong."

The Democratic nominee must accept that Trump is going to get away with unscrupulous behavior. A strategist who worked for Hillary Clinton says, "He's not that complicated. He will not be shamed. He has an incredible pain threshold. You are not going to get him to buckle." She disputes the notion that Trump is a "political genius." Instead, she says, "He is just amoral. He is just a fucked-up individual. So, don't spend a ton of time trying to game out how you can put him in some kind of box."

Amanda Renteria, another Hillary Clinton veteran, says the Democratic candidates must willfully stand up to Trump without reticence or fear. The president is going to attack, Renteria says starkly, and it will be a nasty, personal, maddening, and demeaning experience for the Democrats. Politicians are by nature a defensive and prickly breed, and more than most, they dread being held up to ridicule. The contenders must toughen up, steel themselves, and keep humor and perspective front and center.

A 2016 Hillary Clinton veteran recommends that the candidates ignore Trump's personal attacks but jump to defend his other targets. "Don't go down the rabbit hole with him. When he attacks you personally, do not respond," she says, but "only respond when you're in a position to defend someone else. That was our takeaway from watching the Republican primaries. We never had Hillary respond when he attacked her personally. But you do step in and defend people when he attacks them."

Adrienne Elrod, who also worked for Hillary Clinton's campaign, says that trying to respond to a Trump charge by litigating facts is usually doomed to fail. The press will care more about the fight than about the truth. Calmly and matter-of-factly put out your best response through a spokesperson. No matter how many times and ways Trump attempts to keep the attack alive, she argues, just say you have addressed the matter and refer back to your original statement. Elrod thinks the media, and Trump, will get bored hearing the same answer over and over and will move on to the next skirmish. Hillary Clinton's campaign had a challenging time mastering this approach, especially over her use of a personal server for her State Department emails. When Clinton engaged with Trump, she was forced onto the defensive and became a pawn, and when she stuck to her own message of the day, the media largely ignored her because they found it less exciting to cover.

Moreover, no matter how much muck he throws, Trump will be able to pull rank by virtue of his office. Brace yourselves, says Renteria, and accept that Trump does not influence the environment for the campaign—he is the environment. This is more true now than it was four years ago. "He is the incumbent," she says. "In some ways he gets to set the rules more than in 2016. He has a heck of a lot more in his toolbox. He can take a sudden trip overseas, for example. It is going to be ugly. It is going to be intense. It is going to be hard to stay on the high road."

The election fight will be like a boxing match, Renteria posits, with Trump the eight-foot-tall world champion, who not only boxes but does martial arts and occasionally whips a knife out of his shorts. The challenger will be in the ring alone, with no one to help. If the challenger feels paralyzed, she or he will be knocked down. If the challenger loses a round, the focus must instantly be on the next round. If the challenger wins a round, same thing. The only way to get better at fighting Trump, says Renteria, is to fight him more, hone those brawler's instincts, and feel what it is like to get hit. The candidates cannot hover gingerly outside the ring all winter. If they do not spend the first half of 2020 sparring with Trump as often as possible, then when the entire country starts paying attention next fall, the nominee will have learned nothing about how to land punches and survive blows.

"It's mental, it's physical," Renteria warns. "Folks are going to be stretched a million times. You have to stop saying, 'I can't believe this is where the country is.' You don't have time to be shocked or surprised. It's learning instincts and being able to react in that moment." This will be especially tough, she says, because politicians are used to fighting other politicians, whose actions are traditionally governed by a common set of restraints. Those do not exist with Trump. "He has zero boundaries," she states. "He doesn't have that little voice in [his] head saying, 'Can I actually achieve this? Is this legal? What did I say last week?'"

And, the strategists agree, the Democratic candidates cannot hit back wildly, or try to match Trump's strange amalgam of frenzy and nonchalance, or stoop to his level. They must strike effectively and block blows, while consistently delivering their central campaign messages to the voters. It will be a massive, complicated, disorienting effort. Advisors can help by writing strong lines and crafting counterattacks in advance. One strategist suggests that the nominee designate a staffer to handle all tweets and talking points when Trump engages in down-and-dirty combat.

Mike McCurry believes any candidate with a real shot at the nomination has to spend time in the winter coming up with a list of thirty or so message-based stunts to reclaim space in the news cycle on days when Trump tries to hijack all the attention with an early morning tweet or on-camera comment so outrageous and provocative that the media swoons. Fallon, meanwhile, suggests appropriating a classic Trump trick of feuding with bold-faced names, which usually results in wall-to-wall media coverage. Whenever Trump is attacking an NFL player, a European mayor, a top business executive, or a career politician, the press cannot get enough. Fallon adds that while Trump often chooses human targets to create controversy and distraction, a Democrat can use the technique to stay on message. Rather than make an attack on the banking industry in general, pick a specific CEO to call out. Rather than simply demand that Facebook be broken up, personalize the cause by name-checking Mark Zuckerberg.

And as Tad Devine observes, "Tone is going to matter almost as much as substance in a war against Trump. You are going to have to find the right tone and say the right things." And even if the candidates find just the right balance, they will still rouse ire, make errors, and alienate voters. Doug Sosnik cautions that the nominee must assume Trump will create the same dynamic as in 2016 and turn off a large swath of the public on the electoral process, leaving a great number of voters disenchanted with both candidates.

This is true in politics and in life. Not everyone is going to like you. So run on a message that represents your core beliefs and your heart, and do not stray too far from that essence. The strategists say the Democratic candidates should remember this truth as the campaign heats up and the rhetoric gets messy.

"You must have people around you who remind you every morning when you wake up, 'Look, this is what we're trying to say,'" John Sasso urges. "'A day we do anything that doesn't reinforce our basic qualities, that doesn't draw the contrast with him in a straightforward, dignified, strong way, is a day that we're not winning. We cannot sink to his level. He's the best at that level. If you get into name-calling, if you get into bitterness, if you try to say things that are untrue, just to change them later, he will win that battle every time. If it's a choice between, even somebody who's not going to stoop quite to his level but looks like they're playing his game, you will lose, because you can't beat him at that game. He defined that game, he created that game at the national level. And you're not going to defeat him by doing that. You have to show a contrast in personality.'"

"Remember who you are," says another veteran of multiple presidential runs. "Remember what you stand for. If you do that, nothing can touch you. Not even Trump. Hold your head high and tell him, 'Do your worst.' Then fight against Trump, but fight *for* the American people."

CHAPTER THREE
CANDIDATE REPUTATION

LESSON: PUBLIC IMAGE
IS EVERYTHING.

In the history of the United States, only one Democrat has run against Donald Trump. Yet how much Hillary Clinton's 2016 campaign can teach us about 2020 is a matter of some debate.

A few of Clinton's advisors interviewed for this book feel that her situation was unique in so many ways there is little to take away for the next Democratic candidate. But other experts believe an important, if obvious, lesson was learned: the only opinion that matters in a presidential election is that of the voters. Clinton, sour with the press, tentative with citizens, leery of her own party, allowed herself to be represented by her failings rather than her achievements, and let Trump seize control of her public image.

"Donald Trump's greatest power is his ability to label people and define them," says Anita Dunn, a veteran of the Bill Bradley and Barack Obama presidential campaigns and an advisor to former vice president Joe Biden for 2020. "It's really amazing how good he is at this. If you go back and read *Vanity Fair* profiles from the 1980s, he was doing it even then. He's had a lot of practice."

Trump also had an easy target in Clinton. She already had endured decades of vilification from Republicans and gratuitous loathing from members of the populace. Then in 2016, she declined to put to rest questions about her private email server, the controversies connected to her family foundation, her issue position changes, her husband's personal past, and her health. Nor had she ever been particularly adept at moving on from negative story lines, and Trump instinctively knew how to turn that to his advantage. He was able to present Clinton as an unacceptable choice for some, and as the greater of two evils for others.

Trump's capacity to get away with questionable behavior is singular; no other public figure seems able to make such mischief without lasting consequences. He is like a child caught shoplifting, then allowed to keep the candy, which he was refusing to relinquish anyway. Hillary Clinton, meanwhile, is uniformly treated with suspicion even when her actions are innocuous. Obviously gender is a factor here; the sexism Clinton faced in both her 2008 and 2016 races was glaring. But gender does not provide a full explanation for how Clinton became a cartoon in the eyes of so many Republican and centrist voters. And the last three candidates who challenged incumbents, all men, saw their images hijacked by the opposition and lost because of it.

In 1996, Bill Clinton's team found a way to undermine and redefine his Republican presidential challenger. The GOP had tapped Kansas senator Bob Dole, the austere but respected Senate Majority Leader, as its nominee, and he was seen as a solid choice and a potential threat. Dole, Midwest-wholesome and a star athlete in his youth, had served honorably in World War II, where he sustained grievous injuries and won two Purple Hearts and the Bronze Star, then spent an auspicious four and a half decades in Congress, with nearly thirty years in the Senate. At this time, in the 1990s, such political experience still was considered an advantage for a presidential candidate, and Dole's congressional record was notably moderate and centrist, with a history of bipartisan cooperation. But by November 1996, after months of clever redirection, the Clinton campaign had fused Dole's image with that of Newt Gingrich, the conservative Speaker of the House. Gingrich had helped his party take back the House in the 1994 midterms, a historic victory for the Republicans following four decades in the minority, but caught up in his own newfound glory, the Speaker exchanged power for petulance, engineered unpopular government shutdowns, made some PR missteps, and gave the Democrats an opening to blight the Republican leadership as a unit, presenting the Kansas senator as unpalatably extreme. Dole lost the presidential contest in a landslide.

In 2004, the increasingly unpopular George W. Bush was facing a tough reelection fight against John Kerry. Kerry, like Bob Dole, had an impressive political resume, with two decades in the Senate from Massachusetts and a long stint in the national spotlight. Kerry's war record in Vietnam, moreover, had always been viewed as a political asset. He had enlisted in the Naval Reserve and served as an officer in charge of a swift boat, earning a Silver Star, a Bronze Star, and three Purple Hearts during his short tour. Then, disillusioned by the futile carnage, he renounced the war at a congressional hearing and a public protest. This combination of brave hero and principled activist was hugely appealing to his Democratic brethren, and created an additional threat to President Bush, whose own Vietnam-era military experience in the Air National Guard was dubious and vague. In May 2004, a group calling itself the Swift Boat Veterans for Truth, backed with funds from a Bush ally, launched a relentlessly negative campaign against Kerry, maligning his courage, his military record, his veracity, and his patriotism. The Kerry camp, slow to react against the bewildering onslaught, saw their candidate's finest hour darkened and his reputation tarnished. In a close contest, the attack cost Kerry the race as much as anything else.

In 2012, Mitt Romney, a man who, after achieving a dazzlingly successful career in business, had devoted much of his life to charitable giving and public service, was transformed by the bloodlessly efficient Obama campaign into a callous, greedy real-life Gordon Gekko, villain of Oliver Stone's film *Wall Street*.

Dole, Kerry, and Romney, all solid leaders and strong presidential candidates, were largely caricatures by the time they were judged on Election Day.

For a political candidate, the struggle to control one's public image starts the moment she or he enters the race. Politics is a dirty business, and reputation is everything. As one famous old story goes, when Lyndon Johnson was in a tight congressional contest in Texas, he suggested his team float a rumor that his opponent was copulating with pigs. After his campaign manager protested that no one would believe such a tale, LBJ purportedly replied, "I know, but I want to make the sonofabitch deny it." These days, the task of protecting the candidate's image is exponentially more difficult. Modern information moves at the speed of light, and major damage can be done with a single tweet. Every tidbit of negative press—whether it be an Instagram post or an evening news exposé or a column in an alternative weekly or a front page story in the *New York Times*—is blasted through the same social media loudspeaker. Nothing stays hidden, and everything makes a splash.

In 2020, the Democratic challengers are proceeding with extra caution. They know that Trump is a star political linebacker, skilled at hitting an opponent's reputation, and he has had an entire off-season to get ready. They also are aware that disinformation on social media from sources foreign and domestic can pull the strands of a negative thread unless detected and refuted with the utmost haste, efficiency, and finesse. Candidates lining up to face Trump have sounded the alarm with their advisors, and many campaigns have privately acknowledged that staffers already are taking steps to fight back instantly and aggressively, no matter the source of the story or the outlandishness of the accusation.

Absurd claims that might have been ignored in previous generations, such as the charge that Hillary Clinton was running a secret pedophilia dungeon in the basement of a D.C. pizza parlor, are today recognized as existential threats and must be addressed before they become part of the campaign tapestry. "Candidates now are scared to death that stuff will resonate," says an advisor to a leading candidate. "They've watched what happened to John Kerry and the steady drumbeat of 'lock her up' against Hillary Clinton."

One safeguard, say the strategists, is to start early and build up as much positive, accurate, and demonstrable biographical information as possible, and let it take root in the public's mind. The more the voters know about the history and qualities of a candidate, the harder it will be for new negative information to usurp or subsume the established impression. "Define yourself early on, so there is something people are bumping up against when they are getting that [false] information," says an aide to another presidential candidate. "We are doing everything we can as early as we can so it is there. You need to develop a strong social media presence to build yourself up." This is a challenge even for the better-known candidates, especially in such a crowded field, when most Americans are simply too busy and indifferent to study every wannabe's profile months before they go to the polls.

Still, it remains vital for each campaign to establish its candidate's persona on Twitter, Facebook, Instagram, and other leading social networks in order to create an electronic paper trail, to have a reliable narrative in place, and to give the jittery principal some confidence that his or her best self tangibly exists in the world. In this way, a candidate can have an effective tool to define his or her brand, and to an extent, define Trump. It will help raise money. And it will impress the media.

Democratic strategists believe that last point is key. The press has many biases, but in presidential campaigns, it is biased in favor of competence and strength. The mainstream media may, as an entity, dislike Trump and his policies, but it will still fall prey to the schoolyard lure of watching a playground fight and clamoring for blood. In a one-on-one brawl, if Trump discombobulates his general election opponent, the press corps will participate in shaping the public image of the Democrat as lost, weak, and alone. An online identity as an "It" candidate can help protect against this meme.

How to become an "It" candidate online? The strategists have no definitive answers. Plenty of candidates put up pretty pictures and sincere messages and cutting-edge media, and remain untrafficked, invisible. Some manage to post a few viral clips and then burn brightly until they run out of oxygen. Others are able to parlay their online success into sustaining brands that continue to pull in money and followers and votes. In 2004, Howard Dean used meetup.com to raise cash and demonstrate grassroots support. Four years later, Barack Obama summoned an army of fans on Facebook. In 2016, Trump turned Twitter into an indispensable election weapon, with millions of followers discussing his every tweet. A candidate's success as a social media presence is an ineffable, organic occurrence, an indicator of a sort of mystical digital charisma. Some of the experts suggest that youth is a factor, pointing to Barack Obama's appeal. But that does not explain why cranky septuagenarian Bernie Sanders has enjoyed Internet stardom, or why Donald Trump's social media power dwarfed that of bright, fresh Marco Rubio in 2016.

For many observers, Trump's Twitter usage is a junky obsession, a national embarrassment, and a degradation of the Oval

Office. But the strategists say his thumbed-in missives offer some valuable lessons. Sure, he uses the platform to bully, lie, and threaten. But he also uses it to show his personality, comment on the latest news, and applaud finer actions that occur around the world. He is active, consistent in tone, true to himself, and invariably interesting. He is spinning a never-ending story, and his followers—and many antagonists—are always eager to find out what will happen next. The bond he has created not only is reinforced with each new tweet but extends to reach a broader audience.

Democratic candidates can develop their own social media cortege and distinctive voice throughout the winter, and then, like Trump, use their chosen platforms to project positive traits and biography, needle their opponent, and defend their image when it comes under attack. But first they will have to convince voters to follow their story—as laborious a task as enticing viewers to sample the pilot episode of an obscure Netflix series—and then maintain a narrative so compelling and personal that voters get hooked.

The strategists say that cultivating this kind of brand has outstripped the old-school policy plans and dry multi-point proposals that campaigns painstakingly draw up and few citizens ever read. "It's really important to forge an emotional connection with voters," Mark Mellman says. "More important than an issues package." Explains another veteran strategist, "It's like the old question about who the voters would rather have a beer with. It's now who the voters would rather have living on their phones. They have to get to know the candidate. It's not about who will do a better job anymore. Obviously."

In this way the Democrats not only can allow the voters to virtually meet them and like them, but can offer a contrast in temperament that, for some persuadables, will be welcome. As Obama's chief strategist, David Axelrod, says, a challenger can project a refreshing calmness and stability for those who are exhausted with the daily drama of *The Trump Movie*, as well as a comparable strength. A strategist working for a Democratic candidate says, "For anyone who wants to break out of the field, you have to show that you can take Trump on effectively. So people can envision you on that debate stage against him, that you are tough enough to get through the general election."

As the Democrats define and shape their brands, and try to display their fortitude and good sense, it is essential that they be ready to play defense from the starting gun. Obama campaign spokesperson Ben LaBolt says the Obama reelection effort was the best organized campaign he ever worked on in large part because they had the head start that comes with incumbency and were able to plot and execute different scenarios, the same luxury Trump has now. In a close election, says LaBolt, that time advantage is a huge asset, as Team Trump can figure out how best to define the opposition and plot sabotage while the Democrats are busy fighting it out. In 2012, the Obama campaign peddled opposition research to news organizations in an effort to force Romney to move to the right (locking him into damaging positions for the general election), or create problems for him with conservatives based on past moderate actions and statements. They also had the resources and time to test all manner of different messages and advertisements to use against Romney once he became the nominee.

LaBolt said the Obama reelection effort was able to "start to set a narrative that if you repeat it over a year and a half, it is much more effective than repeating it over three to five months." And that is what the Trump campaign has been doing, coordinating presidential statements from the White House that ricochet through the media, into targeted advertising on Facebook, Twitter, YouTube, and other social media platforms.

So how can the Democrats protect themselves? The first step, basic and obvious, is for each campaign to collect all the damaging elements of the candidate's past—personal lapses, controversial votes, embarrassing gaffes, foolish statements, professional missteps—anticipate how it all will be weaponized, and prepare a defense. Opposition research on one's own candidate is performed by every serious campaign, of course. But for reasons both human and practical, campaigns rarely do a good job at this task. Several of the strategists explain that it requires a candidate to fully empower and trust an aide with the entire process, which can be awkward and complex. Candidates as a breed are defensive, suspicious control freaks, and tend to be delusional about what will and won't be revealed during the course of a campaign battle.

Self-opposition research also requires a sizable budget and staff, and sufficient time to discuss the data in all its private, embarrassing, revelatory, threatening discomfort. The senior campaign staff will need to have candid conversations about how to handle material about the candidate, as well as damaging information about the candidate's family and closest associates. "That's always fun," says one advisor dryly. "Talking to the candidate about how their kid got busted for drugs or posted an inappropriate picture on Instagram."

"The hardest conversations I've had with people thinking about running for president involve self-examination," says John Sasso. "I always say to them, 'You really need to look at everything hard with somebody you trust. Not me because you don't know me and you shouldn't trust me, but somebody you trust who has good political judgment, who has got political antennae, and you must reveal even the most embarrassing and sensitive things because it will come out. And if you talk about it with somebody you trust, who has judgment about these things, you can figure out how to deal with it.'"

Strategists say they have seen this time and again. Candidates are always reluctant to reveal everything about their pasts, even to their closest advisors. They are human beings, who fervently hope that the worst will not come out, and sometimes even wipe whole incidents from their own minds as a defense mechanism. Meanwhile, the aides are forced to press and cajole and admonish. "What are you going to do to deal with what inevitably in this environment is going to come out?" Sasso asks. "Deal with it now. You know, 'that thing I did when I was, you know, twenty-eight years old, it's never going to come out.' And of course it always does. I mean, getting the candidate to recognize that—sometimes you have to jump up and down on the table. It is important, the first important step, and then figuring out how to deal with it."

It is a basic rule of politics: candidates need to know at least as much about themselves as do their opponents. In 2020, this will be an exceptional challenge. Any prospect who has some success after the caucuses and primaries get underway is going to be caught in a vise between their Democratic rivals and the White House and its allies, who will have a shared mission to stop anyone from getting the nomination quickly. Republicans will cheekily echo any resonant attacks, even those made by the far left of the Democratic Party. Trump himself will have the means, incentive, and temerity to unearth and brandish every tawdry detail. Thorough self-opposition research will be a necessary expense, even if the large pack of Democratic candidates may not have the lavish budgets of the well-funded Hillary Clinton and Barack Obama campaigns.

Once the candidates have exhumed their basest selves, choices must be made about when and how to reveal the ugly truth. "Do it right away," insists one operative. "Before someone does it for you. Control the nature and timing of the release. Be honest, be straightforward, answer plenty of questions, don't get frustrated or defensive. It's part of who you are, so own it. Incorporate it into your story. Turn that page."

In July of 1987, Kitty Dukakis, the wife of presidential candidate Michael Dukakis, revealed in an interview that she had previously sought treatment for a long-running addiction to prescription diet pills. Thirty years ago, this sort of disclosure came with a share of controversy, rather than the shrug it would produce today. The decision to preemptively release the information, rather than wait for a rival campaign or news organization to surface the material, was not an easy one. It subjected Mrs. Dukakis and her husband to intense scrutiny at the time when he was just introducing himself to a national audience. But several strategists said telling the story on its own terms helped the campaign by allowing it to frame the disclosure as voluntary and cast the facts in the best possible light.

Advisors say that, in a campaign, honesty is also important internally. Staffers who are on the road or at a desk seventeen hours a day, getting no sleep, separated from their families, accepting minimal pay, need to believe the sacrifices are worth it. They want mutual trust and respect with their leader. Several strategists pointed to Clinton's September 2016 bout with pneumonia, which she concealed for days and only revealed after collapsing in public. "It was a huge psychological and psychic blow for that team," says one person in close touch with the campaign. "They were working so hard, Trump was such a nightmare opponent, and then they felt totally betrayed."

"This is another situation where you have to remember who is on your side," says another strategist. "Your staff wants you to win. Everybody makes mistakes, some are small, some are big, some are huge. But any supporter or voter who expects perfection is a hypocrite or a kook. So put your whole self out there and let your team help you. We aren't the enemy."

* * *

Who, then, is the enemy? In politics that can be tricky to identify. In one of his more grievous attacks, Trump has called the media "the enemy of the people." This statement is both grossly untrue and an assault on American democracy. But the press corps is made up of human beings who are not without personal bias, and over the past several decades, the standards of objectivity, once so carefully tended by most reputable journalists, have loosened considerably. Each day, says Doug Sosnik, the media is going to try to define viable candidates with the most negative story lines and themes possible.

Of course, the press should never reveal a preference for a candidate in a presidential campaign but only report the facts with transparency and precision. Yet many of the strategists interviewed for this book said they detected a clear favoritism in recent nomination battles and general elections. The bias is not always ideological in nature. Instead, the press tends to cheer for the candidates who create a better story and rack up victories. They also reward candidates who not only give them access but win them over personally—access alone is not enough, the strategists say. The candidates have to individually charm the journalists, columnists, and news executives whose patronage they want to earn.

This dynamic has gotten worse over recent years, dismaying old-school reporters and young journalists who entered the profession in good faith. It is troubling to witness, especially for those who have observed the long and steady decline firsthand. The job requirements of the press corps should be straightforward. Journalists, of course, are going to have private opinions as citizens and as human beings, yet they should cover every candidate equally, conveying policy positions, records, values, biography, and character without a hint of partiality.

But that is not the way it works. Bill Clinton beating George H.W. Bush was a better story than Bush 41 being reelected, and Clinton gave his traveling press corps plenty of quality time, during which he was a jovial, garrulous, solicitous companion. Eight years later, George W. Bush enchanted the national press corps with his dry wit and breezy magnetism, and impressed with his macho fundraising show of force. Then John McCain burst onto the scene, holding electric town halls in New Hampshire, hosting reporters on his famous "Straight Talk Express" bus, blowing up the Granite State primary in a landslide, and becoming the undisputed darling of the media, whom he laughingly called his "base." Bush recovered by besting the Arizona senator in South Carolina and had the press back in his pocket by the time he began his general election run against Al Gore.

Gore suffered from a charm deficit in 2000, and the press reacted by focusing on process stories and his political and personal fumbles, rather than on his policy ideas or multitude of positive credentials; many strategists cite the coverage of Gore's presidential bid as a prime example of media bias. In 2004, John Kerry's patrician bearing and aloof mien similarly alienated the media, and the press dove headfirst into the rapid currents of the Swift Boat controversy, despite its unsavory origins and featherweight merit.

Barack Obama perhaps received the most favorable press coverage in the modern era when he first ran in 2008. Hillary Clinton, originally considered the frontrunner and the next in line, was swept aside by the party and the media, which had never considered her likable enough, and she, as did Gore and Kerry before her, found her foibles over-covered and her substance overlooked. When McCain launched his general election bid against Obama, he was stunned to discover his media "base" had deserted him for greener pastures. The story of the brilliant, handsome, charismatic young senator, Hawaii-born, Ivy-educated, Chicago-seasoned, who could be the country's first African American leader, was far too delicious for the press to pass up. Obama tossed out enough dazzling grins and cocksure asides to keep them on his side all the way through his victory speech in Grant Park.

Although the media infatuation had waned somewhat by 2012 when Obama ran for reelection, Mitt Romney offered the press no magic, and for all his eager intelligence and earnest ambition, his staff found that getting him consistently positive coverage was impossible. Romney attempted to court some journalists, but his innate formality and reserve made him seem unapproachable even in the most casual of settings. "A lot of media types had soured on Obama personally," says an advisor. "He was kind of aloof. And they didn't even think he was that great a president. But they didn't like this stiff, Goody Two-Shoes either. Poor Mitt. And they didn't like the narrative of the first African American president being a one-termer." Romney was handily routed in November.

And then came Trump.

The media never fell in love with The Donald. There were no blushes, no swoons, no coy sighs. He was too vulgar and crude and politically incorrect; his biography glittered with a tacky gold plate rather than a lustrous organic nacre; he was a product of Queens, Page Six, reality TV. But Trump roused a passion in the press corps that was intense and unquenchable. They "lusted" after Trump, in the words of one strategist. They couldn't get enough of his rule-breaking, cheap insults, shameless self-promotion, and they "fetishized" the outrageousness of his success, which was a far more interesting story than anything else that was on offer in 2016, even the possibility of the first woman president or the return of the Clintons to the White House. One strategist portrays the press's relationship with Trump as an unhealthy romance; you don't have to love someone to desire them.

All the strategists unanimously believe the press was so caught up in the Trump spectacle that they failed collectively to do their job. With few exceptions, nearly every reporter and analyst covering the presidential race assumed Trump had no chance to win and said as much, essentially promising voters they need not fear an actual Trump administration. They could just put their feet up and watch the show until it was time to complain about what Secretary Clinton was wearing to her inauguration.

The press never held Trump accountable for his stunningly vague policy proposals. They rarely dug deep into Clinton's substantive plans, but instead wrote a lot of stories about in-fighting among her staff; the role of Bill Clinton and whether he was too involved or not involved enough; and Hillary's belabored likability shortfall. They held panel discussions about her yoga emails and Jim Comey. Had the media actually thought Trump might win the general, the strategists say, it would have kept its lust in check. It would not have indulged so rapturously in Trump's messianic rallies or gasped so extravagantly at his trash talking.

Trump has received scathing coverage since the day he took office. There is no doubt that his relationship with the mainstream media is pure antagonism. But the strategists worry that the Democrats might nominate someone who fails to inspire or engage the press, and that reporters will be so intrigued by the idea of Chapter Two of Trump's impossible presidency that the challenger never gets a full voice in the national conversation.

It is imperative, the experts say, that the media come to believe that the story of beating Trump is a better story than the tale of Trump winning reelection. In early winter, once a candidate has established that unassailable brand and strong online narrative, it will be time to craft a heroic tale that starts in Iowa, rolls through New Hampshire, Nevada, and South Carolina, and crescendos when the nomination is secured. The nominee must be the star of the show, the rest of the Democratic field supporting players, and Trump just a loud voice that, from time to time, booms offstage.

The irony, of course, is that Trump is the first person to win the White House in the modern era without a genuine hero narrative to frame his candidacy. He won as an anti-hero. And so this is yet another example of how the Democratic challenger must meet Trump on enemy turf, match Trump's skills, and then top him and be superior, in all senses of the word.

It may not be fair. It may seem insurmountable. But no one ever said winning the presidency was easy.

PART II
SPRING

"SPRING IS THE TIME
OF PLANS AND PROJECTS."
—LEO TOLSTOY

CHAPTER FOUR
STAYING UNITED

LESSON: DIFFERENTIATE
BETWEEN THE OPPOSITION
AND THE ENEMY.

At dinner parties, on cable news programs, in dentists' offices and art galleries and factories, in op-eds and emails, at supermarkets and ski resorts and PTA meetings, Democrats all across the country are declaring they will do absolutely anything to prevent Trump from causing further damage to American democracy and to defeat him in 2020. Absolutely anything.

But will they?

Many Democratic leaders and citizens acknowledge they were too complacent in 2016 and say they have been galvanized to act this time around, prepared to beg and toil, volunteer more hours, donate more money, organize more efficiently, and actually cast their ballots early or go to the polls on Election Day. Party activists, liberals and moderates, even the candidates themselves, have insisted that any one of the two dozen Democrats who entered the race this cycle would make a better president than Donald Trump, and have vowed to maintain a united front against the only opponent who really matters.

That sounds virtuous, doesn't it?

The strategists greet these promises with a dollop of skepticism and a dose of cynicism. They do not doubt that many left-leaning Democrats and independents are making the claim in good faith. But what happens if Democratic donors with Wall Street ties are asked to back an avowed socialist whose policies might have a direct impact on their quality of life, while Trump only causes them psychic distress? Or if activists on the far left, who have spent decades fighting for their deeply held political principles, are pressured to bend the knee and cheer for a moderate, go-along-to-get-along establishment centrist? What happens when Democrats fall into their usual messy pattern of infighting, one-upmanship, and dissonance? As Will Rogers famously put it, "I'm not a member of any organized political party. I'm a Democrat."

Polls have shown that a majority of Democratic voters care more about electability than ideology, but those results beg two questions the party has debated for months. First, what philosophical positioning will make a candidate most electable—a traditional centrist or an advocate of sweeping change? And second, what can be done to placate the party minority for whom ideology is more prized than electability?

And here is a third question: How important is a unified party, anyway? The answer to this one is clear. *Very*. Democrats need to prove they can put forth a tough and worthy competitor who brings the party and the country together while creating a distinct contrast to the chaos of Trump. Of course, nomination battles always get angry and ugly; it is natural for tensions to be heightened as competitors fight for such a meaningful prize. "Divisions are going to occur because it is a Democratic primary," says one strategist. "Most of the candidates are in agreement on the big issues. They don't agree on how to get there, but everybody agrees on almost all issues, which means that the fights will become small and divisive around personal or personality or stylistic differences." But just because the fights will be small and petty doesn't mean they will not do major damage.

The Democratic contenders cannot spend winter and spring squabbling over party semantics, outing each other's bad votes and personal choices, or otherwise kicking mud, pulling hair, and blackening eyes. Such behavior will hand over a load of ammunition to Trump, and yield a weakened nominee by summer. And most critical, it will turn off voters. If young people, activists, and social moderates are not inspired by the nominee and comfortable on the team, then they will not go en masse to the polls, and the Democrats will not have the numbers to get to 270. Several strategists expressed hope that since the stakes are so high, the Democratic campaigns will concentrate on policy distinctions and a shared critique of Trump, while eschewing personal attacks on each other and on the legacy of Barack Obama. But the strategists are not optimistic; they too acutely remember the dispiritedness and disharmony from the last time around. As Donna Brazile says simply, "Unity is the key to our victory. In 2016, we were not unified."

Trump, meanwhile, almost certainly is going to have a united, animated conservative movement and Republican Party standing solidly behind him, no matter the volume of starkly racist tweets or undignified taunts he disgorges from the Oval Office. So many times, Republican voters and groups have idled by, or looked the other way, as Trump has pushed the bounds of decency.

"I could stand in the middle of Fifth Avenue and shoot somebody and wouldn't lose any voters, okay," he said during the 2016 race, and while that assessment perhaps veered toward hyperbole, he certainly has tested the bounds of loyalty. He has welcomed opposition research from a hostile foreign power, imposed tariffs that hurt many of his most ardent backers, and pushed his bigoted statements in the faces of suburban voters. Yet even the Republican officeholders who privately express dismay at his political choices, personal antics, and affronts to the reputation of the party publicly defend and embrace him. Trump fully controls the Republican National Committee and its state parties. The National Rifle Association, evangelical groups, many military veterans alliances, agriculture organizations, and business associations are in his thrall. And his approval ratings among Republicans have been at record highs.

Given Trump's conduct, this is extraordinary. But it is historically consistent with the GOP, whose politicians, voters, and interest groups tend to fall and stay in line more than their Democratic counterparts. To quote Will Rogers again, "Democrats never agree on anything, that's why they're Democrats. If they agreed with each other, they'd be Republicans." President Trump can expect to spend next to none of his time making sure he has a united and energized base going into November, and for any candidate, this is an enormous boon.

The Democrats will have to figure out how to address this imbalance posthaste. Tad Devine, who worked for Bernie Sanders in 2016, says plainly, "You have to put the party together as soon as possible." One need only look to the Sanders campaign to see the dangers. The Vermont senator was as committed to running an issues-based campaign as any major candidate in the modern era. He did not air a single television ad mentioning Hillary Clinton by name or using her likeness.

He did, however, run a TV spot criticizing Goldman Sachs, from which Clinton had received some well-publicized speaking fees. Clinton's campaign saw the ad as a direct condemnation. And in the heat of the competition, Sanders highlighted their differences in a manner that at times became personal.

That was more than enough to rile up his supporters, many of whom were still fuming weeks after Hillary Clinton finally locked down the nomination. They went to the national convention in July brandishing a message of opposition to Clinton, much of it intense and derogatory. Press coverage of the early days of the convention spotlighted the divisions in the party, the Clinton campaign's failure to produce unity, and the far left's critique of the nominee as a centrist sellout.

Even after the Democratic convention, a number of Sanders supporters, especially his younger fans, continued their anti-Clinton rhetoric through the end of the summer and into the fall. Many thought of themselves not as Democrats but as Sandernistas, and in November they either sat out the general election or cast their ballot for an alternate candidate such as the libertarian Gary Johnson or the Green Party's Jill Stein. Just as significantly, they withheld the powerful ground-level energy of Sanders' base from the Clinton campaign.

While Sanders eventually endorsed Clinton and spoke on her behalf, and while her loss can be attributed to dozens of factors, some of them self-inflicted, relatively high on the list was her inability to win over those who backed Sanders in the nomination fight.

"We were vulnerable because Bernie had a lot of supporters who didn't trust the party," says Donna Brazile. "And we needed them to turn out. We did not want them to go another way or to stay home. We put a lot of effort into rallying Bernie Sanders' people, but it was hard."

Says one of Hillary Clinton's advisors, "I believe Senator Sanders and his campaign legitimately tried to help our campaign at the end. But it was too late. His supporters weren't willing to turn on a dime and go from hating her to supporting her. [In 2020] we cannot do that." She is, however, realistic. "It would be great if you could convince people, 'let's have the Democratic nominee not get attacked,' but it's not going to happen. Just because we can identify something that happens in the primary as being problematic for the nominee once they get to the general doesn't mean there's a way to stop it from happening."

Ben LaBolt thinks one solution is avoiding "significant character attacks during the primary," since these types of wounds will linger, fester, and become damaging in the general election against Trump, assisting the president with his central campaign strategy. "He hasn't made America great again," says LaBolt, "so he's going to try to discredit the Democratic nominee based on character. We are playing directly into his strategy if we start to question the character of our candidates."

LaBolt also feels strongly that primary bickering suppresses a crucial faction of the Democratic base: the youth vote, which is essential to stoke collective involvement as well as numbers. "I believe it's an underplayed narrative that millennial turnout was soft in 2016. That's a big reason we lost," he says. "We heard a lot about blue-collar voters moving the other way. But I think that if you don't have a younger voting base that is highly motivated to go to the polls, they won't go. And that's a population where they may not say they believe the character attack, but their enthusiasm levels go down and it's particularly dangerous among that demographic, even though they may hate Trump."

The strategists say that the peril is compounded because so much of the party has shifted left; the fissures are deeper and more jagged, the divisions more tangible, and the story line of disunion more irresistible to the press, which then ignores the substance of the campaign, and focuses, near-exclusively, on the conflict. Still, the more optimistic strategists believe that if the Democratic candidates are able to conduct themselves with discipline during the primaries, then whoever becomes the nominee will lead a unified party at the convention in Milwaukee and in the general election in the fall.

The first recommendation from the strategists is for the candidates to communicate regularly with all their allies, those they know slightly and those they know well, especially during moments of controversy. This may be challenging for busy candidates caught up in the high-stakes pandemonium of primary season, yet these relationships demand care and tending. When perceived or actual disputes arise, even longtime comrades and friendly interest groups may feel the grinding influence of cable news or get caught up in diffuse social media hysteria. Left unattended, these controversies can metastasize, but a skillful candidate not only can avoid the appearance of discord but can create a viable persona for the general election at the same time.

For a more centrist candidate, the challenge is to stay on good terms with the left. Strategists point to the positive example of Bill Clinton in 1992. Doug Sosnik explains that it is vital for such a candidate to pursue core Democratic constituencies early on, in part to get them invested in the campaign and in part to give the eventual nominee a little leeway to break with some of the tenets of those groups without causing a dramatic rupture. Clinton, says Sosnik, finessed this delicate operation adroitly.

Before the voting began, Bill Clinton spent time wooing labor leaders, prominent African American politicians, and influential women's groups. He built on a long-standing bulwark he had constructed as governor of Arkansas and head of the National Governors Association, through which he had met and collaborated with many of the left's most significant activists. Not all of those groups openly supported him, but it was just as significant that they did not actively oppose him either.

That gave Clinton the space he required to take various positions that helped him in the general election but were out of step with party orthodoxy, stances such as advocating free trade, backing the death penalty, pushing welfare reform, and declaring that abortions should be "safe, legal, and rare."

Again, the strategists caution that the 2020 campaign poses an elevated risk for dissension within the party, with the factions on the left particularly vocal and powerful. But many Democratic activists—and not only those who are themselves centrists but also operatives who personally embrace progressive ideology and work for left-wing politicians—say that catering to the most liberal elements of the party is risky and unnecessary for candidates running as moderates.

Bill Carrick contends that the vast majority of progressive voters are in fact pragmatic and want to beat Trump more than they seek ideological purity, while other Democratic strategists fear that changing positions to pander to the left will only make it easier for Trump to paint the Democratic nominee as a Marxist-Leninist in the general election.

Party unity may be essential, but never at the expense of general election viability, say the strategists. For example, supporting slavery reparations for African Americans, or taxpayer-funded health insurance for those in the country illegally, may be righteous pursuits, but backing them would be a hazard for a moderate candidate. Those postures please a segment within the party but leave a nominee open to attack in a general election.

John Sasso says that such candidates need to resist giving in to the demands of interest groups out of a sense of vulnerability, or getting caught up in the contradictory agitation of jumpy staffers. "You know, 'the teachers won't be with you if you do this.' You know, 'we can't tick off this constituency or that constituency.' You've got to resist that kind of stuff," says Sasso. The candidates should keep the focus on what they want to convey about themselves as leaders and as human beings, and on "what people are looking for in the next president."

"Remember the gospel," James Carville warns. "Whatever you put up on the air [in the primary process], you are going to see in September. So understand that. You need to stay consistent."

In other words, be principled. Don't pander to the party's outer edges or cave to the pressure of adopting uber-liberal postures. Follow the Bill Clinton model and adhere to the policy positions that formed the initial foundations of the campaign. That will engender respect from the voters, from the press, and even from the majority of the party. It will reinforce the image of a candidate's authenticity and appeal to general election voters. Being "willing to take on constituencies and the orthodoxy of your own party," says Sasso, is one of the most important ways to demonstrate strength. A strong candidate can keep the party together, even if she or he deviates from some left-wing positions and faces heat on Twitter and other media.

To beat Trump, James Carville says, the party needs to "adopt the 2018 strategy for 2020. Let's focus on things that are relevant to people and stay totally focused on that. We ran one play and scored a touchdown. Maybe we ought to run it again. If you look at where we made the gains, it was with suburbanites. There are swing voters in this country. That's where we made gains. By and large, where we did well was in the suburbs."

By reaching out to a broader spectrum of voters—those who are far from hardline Democrats but who view American leadership from a nuanced, nonideological perspective—the Democratic nominee can scoop up enough swing voters who are disillusioned with or just plain repelled by the current administration to hit that magic 270.

"They are not Democrats like I am," observes Carville. "They are a different breed. They don't like Trump. They like a lot of stuff that the Democratic Party is for." What they do like, Carville says, are proposals for features such as baby bonds and federal funding for day care. What they do not like is talk of issues that tend to divide the electorate, such as support for single-payer health care, open borders, the Mueller report, or Trump's ethics.

And, says Carville, they can be compelled to cast their votes as a statement against Trump rather than as a declaration of their full support for his eventual Democratic opponent. "Trump can't win this election," Carville says. "He can't talk his way back into the presidency. The danger is that the Democrats will talk their way out of it."

"People don't want to vote for Trump," Carville adds. "Nothing could be clearer. You just have to give them a comfort level about voting for you. It isn't very complicated."

For a candidate running as an ardent liberal, the challenge is the mirror image. These hopefuls can assume they will have the energy and support of the party's progressive wing. The task is to cultivate the more establishment and centrist elements of the Democratic coalition without sacrificing the principles that animate their candidacies. This can be accomplished by courting business-oriented Democrats, suburban dwellers, and more socially conservative swing voters with appeals around areas of common ground and by emphasizing the shared goal of stopping Trump from running rampant for another four years.

The progressive candidate must make contact with these groups and individuals early on, even with the knowledge that they will surely not offer support to a candidate on the far left without hesitation. But they nevertheless can be primed to join the fold if and when their preferred type of candidate does not win the nomination. The emphasis, say the strategists, needs to be on selling the vision of an unprecedented mobilization of the progressive movement, inspired by the campaign's sweeping agenda. But the idea of an unstoppable movement should be coupled with reassuring signals that the candidate's objective is to be inclusive, to create as large a coalition as possible, and to offer a presidency vastly preferable to another term for Donald Trump.

Even in the inevitable swirl of controversy, the strategists stress the necessity of keeping a confident, positive stance. Tad

Devine acknowledges that the real disagreements between the wings of the party cannot be papered over, but he argues that the areas of ideological solidarity should be emphasized as much as possible—discussing points of agreement rather than pounding elements of disagreement—to avoid giving the Republicans and the media a chance to sow further division.

Every Democrat in the country, say the strategists, should pitch in with this effort. They may not agree with all the game plans and policies churning in the mix, but they must keep their emotions and biases and preferences in check. Ousting Trump is an all-hands-on-deck undertaking. That means that the most powerful people in the party should step up and do their part, too.

LaBolt says that there is a role here for Barack Obama, who has been noticeably inconspicuous since he left office. Obama is not expected to take sides in the nomination fight but might step in and referee when a Democrat makes a character attack on a fellow party member. "Obama is not going to be out there every day, but he could speak out in key moments," says LaBolt, noting that the president already leaned back into the spotlight to warn his party against becoming a circular firing squad in April of 2019.

A number of strategists encourage involvement from other top Democratic dogs, not only party elders but celebrities and mentors who might have influence over younger voters.

Candidates of all types also should court leaders from the environmental movement, the strategists say. Trump is sure to cast environmentalist positions as radical job-killers, so having personal ties to leading greens will carry weight in the general election and allow some flexibility.

During this period, candidates must maintain relationships with the party's congressional leadership and other elected officials as well. Although Nancy Pelosi is unlikely to offer an endorsement until the nomination is imminent, strategists recommend staying in close touch with the Speaker and her team throughout the spring and beyond. Pelosi herself has strong liberal instincts and comes from one of the most progressive districts in the country. But she has made it clear in the context of the 2020 presidential race that the party's chances for national success hinge on candidates and positions that will appeal to more centrist voters, the kind that helped Democrats win enough House seats to allow her to regain the Speaker's gavel in 2018. Pelosi would like to show Donald Trump the door as much as anyone in the party and her judgment is widely respected. She has distanced herself from the Green New Deal, jousted with the most outspokenly liberal members of the House Democratic caucus, emphasized boosting the Affordable Care Act rather than going for a single-payer system, and avoided the label "socialist" for the party at all costs. She has also publicly demonstrated many of the traits the party's presidential nominee will need to take on Trump, exhibiting fearlessness, humor, dignity, and focus.

Senate Democratic Leader Charles Schumer also believes a more centrist presidential candidate has a better chance of winning the White House and carrying more House and Senate candidates to victory. Several of the strategists suggest that centrist hopefuls keep in regular contact with both Pelosi and Schumer at the principal and staff level, in case they are targeted by progressives and require rhetorical cover. If a prospective nominee can keep the two leaders on their side in private, they will be better protected and prepared for a unified message and political operation come the summer and fall. Says one strategist, "I don't think any candidate can [publicly] turn to Nancy Pelosi and Chuck Schumer to say, 'Let's coordinate this,' but that's what I would say to them [in private]. I would say, 'Let's start working together and figuring out how to win in 2020.'"

"It starts with talking to delegates," says Donna Brazile. "It starts with talking to elected leaders. I would find out who all the major supporters of these candidates are and make sure you have relationships with them. One of the things that helped us in 2016 was that, to the extent that Bernie had a handful of members of Congress that supported him, we began to reach out to [them], to remind them that we wanted a unified convention, and we wanted to give them a role. We still had fights. You've got to expect fights. But what we can't do is when we leave the convention, have this loud chorus of people who are not rallying around the nominee."

Brazile reiterates that the stakes are even higher this time around, and the nominee must work hard to win over and show respect for those Democrats who were in opposition during the primary. "You've got to talk," she says. "The last thing the party needs now is to alienate anyone. I remember back in the day when I worked for Jesse Jackson, and everybody thought, 'Well, it's over and Jesse will just go away.' No, Jesse never went away because Jesse's supporters were not going to go away. You've got to continue to engage those supporters. You've got to continue to show up in the same manner in which the candidate who attracted their support, attracted their eye, you've got to continue to be that force that engaged them and inspired them."

But among all the Democratic individuals and groups across the country, the candidates will be best served by staying in contact with . . . each other. This seems like an obvious and sensible approach, but the strategists say it is advice that is rarely followed, and American campaign history is soaked with bad blood that heated to a rapid boil. Presidential bids invariably are tense, fraught, exhausting, and disorienting. A failure to communicate can lead to misunderstandings or hurt feelings that start with the candidates and their spouses, infect the senior advisors, work their way down to staff and supporters more broadly, and become a mess in the media, often ending with a public disclosure that contains all the indignant details and makes everybody look bad.

One veteran strategist feels that all the Democratic candidates should prioritize inter-campaign relationships, no matter how much time is required, to keep connections cordial. "So much of this is personality driven," he says. "Between the campaigns themselves and the candidates themselves. If I think I'm going to be the nominee, those personal conversations, outreach, those types of things, it's insane that that may matter, but the reality is, they are usually not done."

Candidates should follow basic rules of civility and camaraderie, say the strategists. Personally call opponents and congratulate them on victories, staying on the phone long enough to demonstrate sincerity. Send a text if a rival is having a good moment, or more importantly, a bad day. Check in with a friendly note when the cycle hits a temporary lull. Encourage spouses and campaign managers to maintain an ongoing dialogue, too, reaching out to both counterparts and principals.

"They need to keep in touch with each other," says Craig Smith. "A lot of these people have joint friends. They have members of the Senate, they have members of the House, they have state party chairs. They need to keep in touch with those people. They need to be able to call them and say, 'Look, what you're doing isn't helpful.' It's going to be incumbent on the candidates to make that happen."

The 2016 Clinton campaign is not given high marks on this front by many strategists, including some who supported Clinton's effort. Says one consultant, "I think part of the fundamental problem with the Clinton campaign, they believed in data to the exclusion of politics, right? Just, politics, just good old-fashioned politics. You know, opening the circle to a lot of different perspectives."

LaBolt recommends embracing policies of major rivals after they have departed the race to make a statement that "will be motivational to their supporters." Candidates should lavish praise on their erstwhile foes for coming up with a solid plan and highlight aspects of any proposal that are incorporated into their own.

LaBolt also advocates that the candidates, at the end of all the Democratic debates, no matter how raucous, or in their interviews, no matter how testy, repeat a version of the following mantra: *Every Democrat running is better than Donald Trump. Every one of us believes in opportunity for every American and restoring our alliances around the world, and in a basic right to health care. And we all know Donald Trump doesn't stand for any of those things.*

"There is no reason we can't have that refrain repeated over and over during the primaries," LaBolt says, "especially by the [candidates] who have a tendency to get more contentious. That is a good home base to go to, to put things into context."

It will be useful practice, too, because if the Democratic nominee actually wins the White House, she or he will be serving as a leader of all America's citizens. "It will be the candidates' supporters who want to ignite these intra-party passions," says Craig Smith, who has seen his share of contentious nomination fights. "And it's the candidates' obligation to go to those people and say, 'Look, we're all in this together. At the end of the day we're all going to be on the same side, so let's not spend our time with our guns aimed at each other. We have a common enemy. Let's focus on our common enemy as opposed to focusing on each other.' The tone the candidate takes is important in making that happen."

Sebelius urges contenders who fail to catch on to emphasize a message of reconciliation and harmony as they depart the race. "It certainly would be helpful," she says, "if everybody, the moment they dropped out, immediately says, 'I will work as hard as I can to be part of this effort. I want all my donors, I want all my supporters, I want all my interested parties to join this effort.' And that mantra should be repeated over and over and over and over again."

Strategists from across the ideological spectrum agree: for the Democratic candidates, party unity has to be more than just a whimsical goal. It is an imperative. As one veteran operative says, "There is no road map for winning a presidential election if half your base stays home."

CHAPTER FIVE

OPPORTUNITY KNOCKS

LESSON: YOUR BAD
NIGHTS CAN BE BIG NIGHTS.

On January 8, 2008, something nearly unimaginable happened to Barack Obama: he lost.

After achieving a stellar, come-from-behind victory in the Iowa caucuses five days earlier, and savoring a near coronation from the press and the party, the Illinois senator fell short in the New Hampshire primary, placing second to Hillary Clinton. Obama had started the day of the primary with reason to believe he was about to secure another win and be declared the party's de facto nominee; every candidate, Republican and Democrat alike, who has won both Iowa and New Hampshire has sailed easily to the nomination. Clinton had suffered an embarrassing loss in Iowa, finishing third behind Obama and John Edwards, and had consequently slipped far behind in the Granite State's public and private polls. It was widely assumed Obama would seize New Hampshire and she would be toast.

Clinton fought back. She won the primary by four percentage points and reset the terms of the race. It was one of the most astonishing comebacks in modern American political history, rivaling that of Bill Clinton's well-spun, career-saving, second-place "Comeback Kid" triumph in New Hampshire sixteen years before.

Obama's team was concerned. Concerned about the implications of the inaccurate polling. Concerned about the field operation that had failed to deliver the votes. Concerned that Iowa might have been a fluke. Concerned that Clinton, who had entered the presidential race with innumerable advantages that had made her the heavy favorite to win the nomination, would use her New Hampshire win to reassert her dominance.

Presidential campaigns are filled with drama, emotion, tension, too many decisions to make, and not enough time to make them. For any candidate who ends up in the hunt after the voting starts in Iowa, there are inevitably going to be high highs and low lows. That is just the nature of the beast.

But the night of the New Hampshire primary was a particularly low one for the Obama campaign. All the work that had gone into making him a true contender for the nomination was now in danger of being completely undone by Clinton's impressive recovery. Even some of Obama's staunchest advisors were shaken by the result and its potential implications.

Obama demonstrated the preternatural calm that is one of his greatest gifts. He processed and accepted the outcome. He told his campaign staff and his top donors that there was a silver lining: he would now have to strive for the nomination and prove his mettle. "Change is not meant to be easy," he said to his team. "We have to fight for it."

That night, bone-tired, Obama ascended the stage at the Nashua South High School auditorium looking confident and optimistic. There were cheers and chants as he acknowledged the crowd. After his supporters quieted down, the first thing Obama did was congratulate Hillary Clinton on her hard-fought victory. Then he asked his supporters to give her a round of applause.

At no point in his speech did he seem disappointed. He never mentioned the polls that had favored him to win the state handily, or the rapturous expectations of the giddy politico-media world. Instead, he spoke of what his campaign had accomplished so far and what they would all achieve going forward together.

There were many people watching on television that January night who had never seen Obama speak before. The senator knew that most of the viewers at home, busy people from different states across the country, were only vaguely familiar with him, and largely unaware of what the pre-primary polls had forecast in New Hampshire. He took a moment to stand before the crowd, poised, charismatic, resilient, talking with energy and elegance and hope. When he spoke of ending ill-conceived foreign wars and lowering prescription drug prices, he said, "All of the candidates in this race share these goals. All of the candidates in this race have good ideas and all are patriots who serve this country honorably."

Obama's speech was gracious in defeat, upbeat about his circumstances, optimistic about the future. In tone, it sounded more like a speech he would have delivered had he won, and he behaved like a stalwart leader, ready to deal with adversity and the responsibilities of the country. He left ample room for Hillary supporters, independents, and even Republicans to join him on a quest for a better path.

The results were swift and evident. Obama raised more than $36 million in January, establishing what was at the time the one-month record in American history, most of it coming from Internet donations. He earned a series of high-profile endorsements, won some more primary and caucus contests, and eventually gained an insurmountable lead over Clinton. And he established himself in the minds of many undecided voters as a strong and visionary leader with the qualities required to be president.

Twelve years later, with the swell of social media ever growing, there is more of a media bubble around presidential candidates. They check their Google alerts, watch dogmatic political programming on cable news, scroll through their preferred feeds. They become caught up in the illusion that the entire country is riveted by every tiny development in the race, fully engaged with every aspect of their campaigns. But as many of the strategists point out, despite the greater quantity of coverage, it is still the case that the number of Americans tuned into the presidential race starts out small and only grows incrementally over time.

For self-professed news junkies and those in the political world, election day Tuesdays and primary debate nights are appointment TV, breathlessly counted down and covered and analyzed. But most voters barely register that they are happening, and if they learn the next day about some humiliating gaffe or unsparing takedown, they really do not care. Some may find their interest piqued when favored issues come up for discussion, but for many citizens, the nominating process is simply a reality show that other people are watching. The exception is when candidates take advantage of the big nights with the accompanying brighter spotlight and break through to make a permanent impression, one that creates or cements a brand that carries on throughout the election cycle.

Many of the strategists point to Obama's New Hampshire–night speech as one of the best examples of this maneuver, which they say is a key lesson in how to beat Trump. With his Iowa victory under his belt, Obama used his glaring loss in New Hampshire to demonstrate, with grace, that he was still a player in the game, a worthy candidate, and a safe bet.

Says Craig Smith, "You have to be prepared, no matter what the outcome is, to be able to say, 'I did better than people thought [I would]. My campaign is still alive.' On each election night, you have to be able to stand up there and say, 'This is a victory for us'—'us' meaning 'me and my supporters'—in a way that is (a) believable and (b) motivational. You lower expectations, and you go on there and say, 'Look, the polls said I was going to finish fifth, and I finished third, huge victory for us.' You have got to keep your supporters motivated."

In 1992, Bill Clinton turned his New Hampshire loss into a triumph by proving that his campaign was still alive. In 2008, Obama in some ways benefited as much from his New Hampshire concession as he did his Iowa victory, and he showed that it is as important, and in some cases more important, to take advantage of that spotlight when you lose than when you win. "The crazy thing," says Ben LaBolt, "is that a bad night can be as good as a good night. That day was actually a very good fundraising time because there was a big moment of peril for the campaign."

It is critical, adds Smith, for candidates to instantly reassure their supporters at moments of crisis, because if the money dries up fast, then there are no funds to pay for a rebound, the momentum slows, the financial reports are mortifying, and the press smells blood. "You've got to convince your donors that they're not wasting their money, that this campaign is still viable and still alive, it's gaining momentum," he says. "Donors are like everybody. I always say small-dollar donors are like people who go to the horse track. Whether they bet $2 or $2,000, when their horse is coming down the home stretch, and they have got a shot at winning, they're screaming their lungs out. If the horse is coming down the home stretch and ain't got a shot at winning, you know, they are throwing their tickets on the ground."

And it is not only about preserving and inspiring the donors, but using the occasion to tap the wallets of a fresh group who is just tuning in and may be increasingly generous as the race proceeds. One veteran strategist talks about the importance of "maximizing raising money from people that are getting a real eye on you for the first time. The obvious thing would be to raise it among hard-core Democrats, but the less obvious choice would be for data folks to create models of likely supporters in a general election. And see if you can make some progress there, if, say, there's a significant number of people that voted for Donald Trump and then voted for [Wisconsin Democratic senator] Tammy Baldwin. It's actually not that hard to figure out who those people are. So if you were the Wisconsin primary winner, and the local news is filled with 'you're the winner of the primary,' that would be a pretty good opportunity."

In 2020, especially given the large Democratic field, there are likely to be election evenings, some with multiple contests, where the outcome cannot be definitively forecast. But those nights are unquestionably going to help define the race, and the candidate has to be ready to recognize and leap upon an opportunity to make some noise.

Trump is assuredly going to be trumpeting his own election night news. Assuming, as seems likely, the president does not have a major nomination challenge, Team Trump will be able to use the evenings when the Republican and Democratic contests overlap to execute many of the same tasks that the strategists say the Democrats must perform. Trump will exploit the swell of public and media interest to celebrate his results, rev up his base, make an appeal to a general election audience, decry the opposition, and take steps to spur and capture online contributions. And, with no opponent and victory assured, Trump will have had months to prepare for these evenings, with ample resources and the spotlight of incumbency.

The strategists acknowledge that the uncertainties and pressures of any election day, which follow a period of intense campaigning without reprieve, make planning and implementation difficult. But, they say, there are no excuses. "You want to be taken seriously and break out," says one expert. "You have no choice. Put in the time and the money and the staff. These are the nights when history is made."

This planning involves some of the basic nuts and bolts of any presidential campaign. When asked to enumerate the necessary items, several of the strategists apologized. *This stuff is so obvious*, they said. *It is ridiculous that it even has to be pointed out.* But they were nevertheless fairly certain that at least some of the Democratic 2020 candidates would fail to enact all of the tasks, and sheepishly admitted that they had worked on past campaigns that had botched these fundamental moves. And they took a good bit of the blame—it is part of a strategist's job to remind the candidate of the obvious. The checklist may be straightforward but should not be taken for granted.

Choose the right location. Decide if the candidate should speak from a state that votes that night, one with an upcoming contest, or a general election battleground.

Determine the staging. Resolve if the candidate should appear alone on the dais, flanked by family, or surrounded by supporters.

Time it well. Make sure the candidate does not speak too early, before the results are clear, or too late, after the press and the media have called it a night. Most definitely do not speak while the president is talking.

Write it out. Be certain the text of the speech is well conceived, well edited, fact-checked, and locked down (no winging it on these nights, as others have done, to their detriment). Be sure the message inspires core supporters while laying down a foundation to appeal to both Democratic voters in upcoming nomination contests and swing voters in the general election.

Prepare the digital team. Ensure that the message can be amplified, especially if the candidate hits it out of the rhetorical park, and the operation is ready to pull in a massive haul of online contributions. The candidate should help direct traffic to the campaign website, and the signage should be made simple for citizens to navigate and contribute.

All of these elements should be updated for the 2020 technological and social media landscape. While Obama's 2008 methodology was pathbreaking at the time, it is now the stuff of the Internet Stone Age. "We have been running the same playbook for years in terms of content," says LaBolt, "which was just kind of clipping up the best moments on YouTube and putting them out and then maybe trying to get an ad together overnight. I think we want to be on more platforms this time around. I think we want a more sustained content strategy and treat it as a twenty-four-hour exercise. Those key moments are played again and again, and there are some platforms that we haven't fully engaged on yet."

Caucus and primary nights, says another expert, are the time to start trying out new platforms, going beyond Twitter, Facebook, YouTube, and Instagram to services such as WhatsApp and perhaps other networks currently in inception, to reach targeted voters who are less participatory in political social media. In order for a campaign to now take full advantage of pivotal moments and significant nights, it needs to road test production and distribution ideas necessary for the expansion of a candidate's social media profile, for the selection of a running mate, for themes at the national convention, for offensive and defensive strategy during debates, and for last-minute maneuvers in the final weeks of the general election.

And those who win, place, or show in the nomination contests must be ready to introduce themselves as if for the first time, since they will always be new to a segment of the voting public. Again and again, the strategists drive home this point. In victory, candidates must be gracious and unifying, congratulatory of their rivals and inspirational to their supporters. In defeat, candidates must radiate confidence and optimism, put the best face on their results, and project forward to the fights ahead.

"In the early states," says Craig Smith, "you're going to want to still stick with your message that is going to win you the primary. But as the process evolves and you're still viable and alive, you're going to want to shift to a message that becomes somewhat more inclusive and somewhat more general election focused. When you can see your path to victory, and it's a real path, you should start putting some of that [general election message] in there."

Back in January 2008, on the day of the New Hampshire primary, before the results were tallied, Obama stopped by a polling station, where he engaged with some voters who were campaigning for John Edwards. It turned out they were from a steelworkers union, and they were delighted to meet him. They shook his hand and wished him luck, and Obama took his leave. "See you in the general," he said.

CHAPTER SIX
WILD CARDS

LESSON: SPECIAL PROJECTS
COULD DECIDE THE OUTCOME.

F or those in the political-media world, campaign season seems endless. Frantic winter months of frigid, snow-crusted rallies and house parties and town halls and puffer coats and wet boots and yard signs and fresh alliances. Then weeks and weeks and weeks of the spring season, crisscrossing the country, waking up every Tuesday to witness more chunks of the country casting their votes, candidates dropping like flies, fundraising hauls and dribbles, hunts for endorsements. Then hot summer comes, bringing unexpected conflicts, new controversies, and at the conventions, protests, police, revelry, and grand rhetoric. Then the fall, with its sudden surprises and fateful debates and final countdowns. Interminable, exhausting, a life span of drama every day. And for the contenders, there is never enough time.

Even the most organized campaign effort cannot find the hours in the spring for the kind of extensive, systematic, long-term planning required to beat a sitting president in the fall. But the strategists urge Democratic candidates to heed the six wild-card elements that can decide the entire election. Take these steps in the spring, they warn, or ignore them at your own risk.

Wild Card #1:
Disinformation

Democrats believe that Trump's allies, foreign and domestic, will use social media and other digital communication as they did in 2016. They will traffic in false and misleading information to deliberately damage the Democratic candidates, and will attempt to peel off or suppress votes from certain demographics, particularly in African American and Hispanic communities. There have been increased security measures to prevent the hacking episodes that were so detrimental in 2016, but Democratic candidates and their party leaders remain vulnerable to all manner of cyber-attacks and disinformation. The Democratic strategists have zero confidence that the Trump administration is interested in using the powers of the federal government to limit the spread of fallacious narratives that assist the president's own effort.

One longtime strategist is apprehensive about such sabotage. "We don't know how the technology is going to change. We don't know how Facebook and Twitter are going to play in 2020, but we've gotten indications that they're just going to go along and be along like they were in 2016. That hurts credible candidates. All of that hurts credible candidates."

To combat this threat, say the strategists, the nominee must set up a war room to monitor fake and malicious content and respond posthaste. And the campaign needs to allocate significant resources to the project; it can't merely assign a couple of young volunteers with aging laptops and a stash of Monster Energy Drinks, but it should build a complex, analytics-driven operation that locates and exposes questionable messages coming from subterranean sources.

"The rapid response operation has got to be more engaged," says Ben LaBolt, "so it's not just about fending off incoming attacks, but rather sophisticated social listening that documents patterns. If Donald Trump suddenly gets a bunch of African American supporters spreading an anti-immigration message, that's a red flag, and we need to look into whether that's a real effort or fake news that's being spread. I would consider hiring folks who have been monitors for the platform companies to look for those patterns and make sure that they're being quashed quickly."

According to the strategists, one way to counteract spurious stories from the enemy camp is to fill the same spaces with positive messages and anecdotes, as well as with mordant critiques of the president's record, and do so with far more pugnacity than anything attempted in 2016. "We need to set up our own aggressive production studio," says LaBolt. "Somebody who's set an editorial agenda before should be involved in that effort. The campaign should be producing as much content as the [opposition is], and it should be a sophisticated effort across platforms. Not only Facebook and Twitter but YouTube, an advertising effort that's reaching people on Hulu and all the places they consume information. That's on us to produce."

Indeed, do not expect these social media platforms to serve as partners in truth, even in the interest of American democracy. They so far have shown distressingly little initiative to protect their product or tamp down the devilry. Nor do they have the bandwidth to keep up with the volume, speed, and stealth of the outlaw operations, which have only grown in the last four years despite the widespread exposure and condemnation after the 2016 battle. And the attacks will remain one-sided. "Democrats will never stoop to this," says a presidential campaign veteran. "It's just going to be asymmetrical whack-a-mole. You have to fight it as much as possible."

The Democrats can talk publicly about the responsibilities of major social media companies to police their own content, but strategists strongly recommend that the campaigns maintain a private dialogue with the organizations, notifying them of abuses and pressing for redress. Strategists further encourage campaigns to hire some staff members who have worked at places such as Facebook and Twitter, and take advantage of their relationships and institutional knowledge.

Says Jennifer Granholm, "Short of legislation, which we are not going to get in Congress, I think there has to be a very public pressure campaign on the platforms to not allow this crap to come through because it will poison like it did in 2016. They've made some steps. But I do think strategically there has to be a backdoor effort, and a public pressure campaign as well."

Yet the strategists are not the least bit optimistic that these measures will curb the invective or equal the balance in any way. "It's really a losing battle," sighs one Democrat. Says Tad Devine, "You have to factor in foreign interference. You have to be on top of it and figure out how to expose it in a way that is credible with voters. You have to surface it above the radar and have people with integrity and credibility talk about it. Line that up in advance." Campaigns must hire a team of trustworthy cyber security experts who can explain the malfeasance to voters and the press, and push for further public scrutiny and media inquiry.

One strategist notes that purportedly neutral parties must be tasked with holding the platforms accountable, because, while the campaigns are obliged to press for truth, they often are inadequate messengers. "The problem is campaigns don't have any credibility," he says. "I think it is up to third-party groups and the media to say, 'This information being put out there is false.' The more that is out there, the more that they need to say that this is false information."

It still will be difficult, however, to reach the voters who were targeted. "They watch different media, they only get information from a very narrow list of sources that are all pushing the same fake line," the strategist explains. "But I also think that what would be good is a whole effort with Twitter and Facebook, to say to them, 'There is a campaign coming up. And in a campaign, there are a whole lot of things out there that are true and, as we learned last time, there is a whole lot of information being put out there that is not true. So be careful.'"

Meanwhile, the Democratic candidates should always assume that the White House will be busy undermining all these defensive plans, facilitating the mischief, and concealing any collusion. Brian Fallon warns that Trump will once again lay down the melody and let his allies croon the chorus and strike up the band. The president will introduce a line of attack with the full knowledge that his message will be picked up and amplified, harmonized and distorted. And Trump can still avoid incrimination for the more extreme tones, which will reverberate to his benefit without causing him a headache.

So how does a Democrat combat false information, disseminated by unscrupulous minds, unfettered by global platforms, and promoted by the president of the United States? The strategists advise the candidates to take the high road, seek refuge in the equal branches of government, and stay strong together.

"I don't think you match their tactics," Granholm says. "You do not want to be engaged in passing around fake videos, but you do have to have a whole side campaign that alerts people to these fake efforts. 'Look what they're trying to do to you. This is what he's been doing to the American people. He has been conning them and now they're cheating by sending [around] false news stories.' I mean that it has to be part of your campaign about why he's not worthy to be president. 'You don't want a president that won by deception. And that's what he's doing.'"

The strategists have some soothing words as well: do not forget the government is not entirely controlled by Trump. Solicit portions of the legislative and state entities to vigorously identify and expose fakery, and lean on your Democratic allies to be vigilant and present a cohesive front.

Says LaBolt, "We were gun-shy on using investigatory powers in 2016 to investigate fears that the election was being unduly influenced by foreign powers. But, in fact, it was. In 2020 I wouldn't hesitate to get Democratic investigators in Congress to quickly use subpoena power to figure out what's going on. We should move quickly to call hearings and subpoena people. I think Democratic attorneys general in the states should be ready to take legal action. We [Democrats] tend to be very hesitant about pursuing these strategies as a party. We should truly plan for the worst to come at us, and be ready to activate and coordinate at all levels. The campaign needs to organize some sort of a unified strategy."

Wild Card #2:
Voter Suppression

For decades, Democrats have fretted over Republican plots to limit ballot access, agonizing especially over threats to suppress African American, Hispanic, and younger voters. Increasingly, with each election, they have worried that voter intimidation, ballot tampering, and purposefully created confusion will have such a forceful cumulative impact that the election will effectively be decided by fraud. The party is particularly concerned in 2020, because of Team Trump's long-running and well-financed campaign, and because the strategists uniformly believe that the president's operation will push the boundaries of past practices to gain every advantage.

In other words, they think the Trump campaign will bend the rules and break the law to maximize its chances of winning. "Trump has never played by the rules in business or in politics," says one Democratic strategist who works closely with election lawyers. "Why should we expect him to start now?"

It may come as a surprise to many U.S. citizens, but ensuring a fair vote in this country is a challenge. The supervision of American presidential elections is still largely decentralized, making it difficult to safeguard every jurisdiction. There is no cookie-cutter or federal approach that will work uniformly for the nation's nearly three thousand counties, and the avenues for roguery are many. From the passage of new laws or implementation of local regulations that would create obstacles for Democrats to vote, to decisions about election administration, to physical efforts to intimidate voters who cast ballots early or arrive at the polls on Election Day—there is an infinite amount of work awaiting the party's legal team.

Other concerns: voters being purged from the rolls; shifting or unclear requirements for accepting or counting ballots; polling places being moved at the last minute; misleading communications from election authorities; and insufficient planning to deal with long lines, which will be exceptionally problematic if the turnout is unusually high as expected.

Once voters are scared off or confused about casting their ballots, it is difficult to get them back to the booth. A specious notification that voter IDs might be checked at polling venues, for instance, can have a chilling effect on participation. And, as with so much else in a close election, legal efforts to combat these threats can determine the outcome. They also can contribute to whether the declared result of an election is considered legitimate and universally accepted.

Bob Bauer, one of the Democratic Party's most experienced election lawyers, who also served as Barack Obama's White House counsel, says that candidates should prepare for legal wrangling as soon as there is a realistic path to the nomination. As with safeguarding against damage from disinformation, protecting the integrity of the vote will be an expensive and time-consuming enterprise. Says Bauer, "Campaigns need to make an enormous investment—not only a legal investment but a field investment. The most important step that a campaign can take, in my judgment, is to deploy field staff solely concerned with voter protection to the key states as early as possible."

Bauer and other legal strategists strongly recommend that the campaigns make contact between their in-house vote protectors and local administrators long before November, ideally in the spring. "You have to set up in the state, you have to master the legal and regulatory environment. You have to start building relationships, starting dialogue," says Bauer.

The strategists feel such an effort is well worth it, since most election officials, regardless of party, are genuinely concerned with protecting the vote and will appreciate friendly outreach from an experienced lawyer. It takes time, however, to establish the trust and connections required to work through problems as they arise. And if there are election officials in key jurisdictions who are going to be hostile or function as Trump allies, it is best for the Democratic campaign to know that as soon as possible.

"If you are not deploying your vote protection coordinators until the convention, you are making a catastrophic mistake," Bauer says. "There is just not enough time. You want people to build relationships. You want people to be able to call the person in the DA's office who is most responsible, the person in the election administrator's office who is most responsible. You don't want [the field lawyers] coming in in the first instance telling them what to do, yelling and screaming at them. The goal is to get people in the jurisdictions that you're most concerned with who are going to begin to build relations with local election administrators. They are going to keep an eye on what is taking place at the local administrative level. They are going to keep an eye on what state legislatures might be doing. To the extent you can spot those problems early and deal with them early, you are far better off."

There are always some voting complications and disputes, and in 2020, the stakes are sky-high. "No Democratic candidate can win without achieving targeted goals in the African American community. End of story," says an experienced election lawyer. "The [Republicans] know that, and we know that. If you look at any given voting group, the one that obviously they're going to be most focused on are high-density, African American neighborhoods in major cities in targeted states," with potential attempts to purge voters from the registration rolls, or the failure to accommodate long lines. Similar ploys and the spread of inaccurate procedural details could be used to suppress Hispanic and young voters as well. So, say the strategists, what might seem like a costly and dry legal project could, in fact, head off calamity. Says one operative with his own history of dabbling in the darker arts of politics, "No Democrat wants to walk away from 2020 with Trump back in the White House because they fell for the oldest tricks in the book."

Wild Card #3:
The Green Party Challenge

In both the 2000 and 2016 presidential elections, the Green Party, with its little, fierce band of loyalists, took just enough votes to swing the Electoral College and cost the Democrats the White House. During both races, Democrats, complacent and afraid of backlash, made little effort to warn Green voters that supporting their preferred candidate was a dangerous waste of time, or challenge enough petition signatures to nix the Green candidate as an option on the ballot. The strategists say that, in 2020, Democrats cannot risk losing a single Electoral College vote. They will have to persuade citizens who prioritize the environment and reform that a vote for the Greens is a vote for Trump, or consider the drastic step of trying to keep the Green candidate off of battleground state ballots.

You can bet, say the strategists, that Team Trump will do everything in its power to ensure that a Green Party representative gets on the ballot and thrives, by targeting social media, undermining the environmental and reform credentials of the Democratic nominee, and even explicitly bolstering the Green candidate. As in 2016, Trump can increase his chances of winning the election with a two-step move: convince voters that the Democratic choice is just as flawed as Trump, and therefore present Trump as the lesser of the two major party duopolistic evils; and nudge the dissatisfied to cast their ballots for a trendy, inspirational third option in the person of the Green Party candidate.

Although toying with voter rights is hardly in keeping with the Democratic brand, some strategists suggest that the party examine battleground state ballot access rules and perhaps mount challenges to deny the Green candidate a spot. "It's a little shady," admits one strategist, "but these are serious times. The campaign can try to do this, or give it to an outside group and then coordinate behind the scenes."

Even former DNC interim chair Donna Brazile, a longtime champion of expanding ballot access, says that members of her party might not rule out this option. "I don't know if we can keep [the Green Party] off the ballot. I've never seen the [Democratic] Party get in the business of trying to keep people off the ballot, but one never knows." Other experts who, like Brazile, get squeamish at such a thought, say the Democratic candidates should just start early to engage voters who might lean Green.

"I do think we need to communicate with those voters on the issues that matter to them," says one. "I think we have an opening. There is not a Democratic candidate that's not serious about climate change this time around. It didn't come up much in 2016, but there is a series of commitments that can be made in a public-facing strategy." He advises that the candidates "test the messaging and see what works. Telling somebody that they're going to throw the election if they vote for that candidate may not be an effective strategy."

Craig Smith disagrees with this last point. "We as a party need to do a better job of explaining to people that voting for a candidate who has no chance of winning is like throwing your vote away," he says. "The future of democracy is on the line here. So going down there and voting for a third-party candidate is a vote for Trump. I don't think we did a good enough job of doing that in 2016. This time it is going to be much easier to convince those people that third-party votes cost us this many states, third-party votes got Donald Trump elected president. They have lived it, they have seen it. And I think it becomes easier to sell to them."

Brazile, who managed Al Gore's general election campaign, experienced the Green Party threat firsthand, when Ralph Nader attracted money, media, voter devotion, and a political theory of the case, siphoning all four from the vice president. "We saw it in 2000 but ignored it," Brazile says. "[We thought], 'It's not going to happen because people will see the clear difference between George Bush and Al Gore.'"

Brazile believes the Democrats should have learned from Gore's experience, and approached the portent of the Green Party with greater diligence four years ago. The modeling tools used by the Clinton campaign, she says, did not predict that Hillary might lose because of the Greens, and the notion that the Democrats might make the same mistake yet another time is unimaginable. "If we ignore them and don't understand how they cut into our base, we will not have learned the lesson of what I have experienced twice," says Brazile. "Of all the pots, this has to be at the top of the stove, not underneath. This is another issue that has caused us heartburn because we failed to address it in a timely manner." Starting the outreach in the spring and continuing through the convention is essential. "We've done it before," she says, "but that message has gone out in the wee hours in the preelection window, post debates. What I'm saying is that the Democrats have to recognize that this has to be a concern sooner. This has to be part of the messaging going out before the convention, not just after the convention."

The operatives feel that if the Democrats act fast, they can flip the dynamic Trump utilized in 2016, and can sway Greens by pointing to Trump's record on the environment. After four years of Trump, it will be difficult for the Green Party to make the argument, as they did in 2000 and 2016, that there is no difference between the Democratic and Republican Parties, and that there is room for a protest vote or an extreme Green dream.

Wild Card #4:
The 3 Percent Solution

There have been whispers flitting in the air and across the country, passing through cocktail parties in Santa Monica, conferences in Aspen, cafeterias in Chicago, suppers at the Polo Bar, about a plot both daring and near-foolproof that, if executed correctly, would guarantee a Trump defeat.

The audacious scheme calls for the recruitment of several well-regarded, mainstream Republicans, prominent business-people, or former elected officials—say, ex-governor Tom Ridge of Pennsylvania, ex-governor Tommy Thompson of Wisconsin, or former congressman David Jolly of Florida—and then placing them as independents on the general election ballot with the expressed purpose of undermining Trump. Each candidate would offer a record of public or elective ser-vice, a sterling reputation, access to campaign funds through personal wealth or strong relationships with donors, high name identification, and an unambiguous message: *I am doing this to defeat Donald Trump and save the future of the Republi-can Party*. Alternately, a single candidate with a national repu-tation, rather than a series of state-by-state challengers, might make a bid. If Ridge or Thompson, or perhaps Mitt Romney or Massachusetts governor Charlie Baker, got ballot access and ran on the same message in a handful of states, they could po-tentially deny Trump reelection even if they won just 3 percent of the vote.

Given the broad support the president has from the GOP, the candidates and their allies would have to be prepared to take tremendous heat from their own tribe. Still, if the election is as close as expected, a talented and committed challenger could pull enough votes in a battleground state to make it im-possible for the incumbent to win, especially if the Democrats deftly manage the Green Party.

The strategists say that this gambit might hatch inde-pendently after a lively Never Trump confab, but they also note that the Democrats actively can spur such a plan by work-ing with intermediaries and broaching a series of policy and personnel deals to lure prospects into the fray. The ballot ac-cess deadlines are strict and the personal and professional de-mands onerous on whichever Republican maverick or mavericks are tapped for the mission, should he, she, or they choose to accept it. This moonshot project, therefore, requires initiation in the spring. *And this tape/page will self-destruct in five seconds.*

Wild Card #5:
The New Alliances

The progressive biosphere is bursting with fresh grassroots groups, many arising in reaction to Trump, many led by women. Members are local, Internet-savvy, organized, and engaged, and they participated intensively in the 2018 midterms. Campaign staffers in House districts that flipped from Red to Blue report that many of their volunteers were affiliated with these groups and appeared to organically show up for activities such as voter canvassing and outreach. With names such as Indivisible, Sister District, and Swing Left, these groups remain a bit of a mystery and no one in politics or academia has a grasp of how big or influential these alliances will be in 2020.

It is clear that the groups are made up of progressive citizens highly motivated to defeat Donald Trump, and that they will energetically perform activist functions (messaging, voter contact, voter engagement, registration, turnout) at the local level, without the need for marching orders from national headquarters. Yet the strategists say it remains an open question how much more potent these groups might be if given guidance and encouragement by the Democratic nominee.

"We [Democrats] run very top-down operations," says Will Robinson. "What really makes Trump successful is, even though he's got a plan and control, that thing is highly decentralized. We got all these things—Indivisible and other groups—who want to go at Trump, and we need to let them go at it, encourage them. Every time you try to pull people in and give them absolute direction, it doesn't work. The way we are going to win this thing is to operationalize people at a local level. We need our activists to self-publish."

These homegrown entities typically do not boast more than a few hundred members in any given locale, but, as a whole, they are a sleeping giant of organizing energy that could make the difference in a close election. The strategists believe that early and consistent coordination with these groups in the battleground states can pay dividends by creating an army of relatively autonomous supporters that the Republicans cannot match. It is one of the few areas of asymmetry that works in the Democrats' favor.

Say the strategists, all that is required is to assign some campaign staffers to catalogue and boost the groups located in a targeted area. "Don't tell them how to do their work, just give them whatever resources are necessary," says one. That will make them a force multiplier for which there is no analogue, either elsewhere in the Democratic Party or as part of the Trump reelection effort.

Muses another operative, "I think you probably have a designated team that is keeping them up to date, that is providing a list of activations for them, that can help them select the lanes where they'll be the most powerful, that can fight for some level of a cohesive effort. It should be coordinated with the campaign and be additive to the campaign. Some of the potential nominees will speak very well to the activist base, some would not. And if they don't, they are really going to need these groups."

Wild Card #6:
The Supremes

For a stately group of esoteric legal minds, the Supreme Court often is the wildest political wild card of all. It is elementary to predict that something will happen on this front, but it is impossible to predict what that something will be.

The Supreme Court almost always holds its most controversial opinions until the final days of its session, which typically concludes in June or early July. The 2020 docket is set up to include cases involving gun rights, gay and transgender rights, immigration, the Affordable Care Act, and abortion. The strategists admit that there is virtually no way for the Democratic nominee to prepare a full response in advance, but they observe that voters on the right tend to pay more attention to judicial branch rulings than those on the left, and that the media is prone to exaggerate the impact of these decisions on the presidential outcome. The trick is to use the court outcomes to highlight policy proposals and leadership, rather than get bogged down in legal theory.

"While all of the Supreme Court's decisions will be important, and many of the issues it rules upon will be topmost for the Democratic Party base and even some swing voters," says Jill Alper, "health care is likely to take center stage. If the Affordable Care Act is changed or overturned in some material way, the nominee must pivot to focus on solutions and turn that reversal into an electoral argument, not a legal one."

Trump is almost certain to publicly celebrate decisions that go his way and denounce the Justices if he does not like a particular adjudication. It is important, say the strategists, to make sure a team of campaign lawyers is completely familiar with the arguments in each case, and that the team coordinates with the political and communications shops before the decisions are released.

Brian Fallon, who was a senior official in the Obama Justice Department before working on Clinton's 2016 campaign, believes the party needs to put a greater emphasis on issues related to the judiciary generally, not just on the Supreme Court. "The Democratic nominee should not even wait for the rulings to come out next June to decide to run against the Supreme Court," he says. "Invoke its rulings in *Citizens United*, *Shelby County* [a voting rights case], and the gerrymandering case to tell the story of the Supreme Court's partisan capture and its role in rigging our democracy. Invoke its rulings in [union dues case] *Janus*—and the Chamber of Commerce's 80-plus-percent win rate in recent years—to tell the story of the Court's corporate capture and its role in rigging our economy. Talk about how this Court has overturned no fewer than four twenty-plus-year-old precedents in just two years and explain how the Court's conservatives are the new judicial activists, making law from the bench."

Despite Fallon's argument, other Democrats caution not to get so caught up in judicial rulings that the eye comes off of the prize, or off of the real foe. As Alper remarks, "Historically, Republicans have been able to draw a straight line from the Senate to the Supreme Court, whereas Democrats have had more of a challenge, especially during our primaries where voters' 'muscle memory' is built for the [presidential] general election. First and foremost, the election needs to be a referendum on Trump—and that should be the focus of the nominee and the party."

• • •

Unconventional times call for unconventional measures. Any one of these six wild cards could genuinely be the deciding factor in November. Start reaching for these cards in the spring, the strategists warn, or there will be no chance to play them in the fall.

PART III
SUMMER

"SUMMER'S LEASE HATH
ALL TOO SHORT A DATE."
—WILLIAM SHAKESPEARE

CHAPTER SEVEN
NIGHTMARE SCENARIO

LESSON: DON'T LET THE START
OF THE GENERAL ELECTION BE
THE END OF YOUR CAMPAIGN.

In 2011, Republicans thought Barack Obama was doomed.

In the midterm elections the previous year, Republicans netted sixty-three House seats, the biggest shift since 1948. The GOP also took six Senate seats, along with six gubernatorial wins and twenty state legislative chambers.

Obama entered the White House in 2009 with a full agenda and fallout from the 2008 financial crisis; his first two years in office were dominated by a major stimulus package and regulatory tightening, the auto company bailout, and the Affordable Care Act. These enterprises kept President Obama busy but did little to gain favor for him or his cohorts, and after scores of Democratic officeholders across the country lost their jobs, his own approval ratings were as sluggish as the slow-growing economy. When the electorate tilted, it appeared Obama was in substantial danger of being knocked from his perch.

Sometimes, it is said, the appropriate reaction to adversity is panic.

But instead, Team Obama studied history, applied lessons from the reelection triumphs of Bill Clinton and George W. Bush, employed an incumbent's advantages of time and money, and methodically positioned its leader for victory. By the beginning of summer 2012, the Obama campaign was well on its way to implementing a sterling blueprint for reelection, with no nomination challenge, and was more serenely confident of a general election win than any presidential effort in recent history, carrying out its plan step by step.

Step One: Early fundraising. The Obamas began collecting small-dollar and large-dollar contributions right away, so the campaign would be flush, donors would be psychologically and financially invested, and the president, a notoriously reluctant supplicant, would be freed up to focus on campaigning by the start of 2012.

Step Two: Reconnect with the base. The campaign reestablished ties to longtime supporters, some of whom had expressed disappointment with his presidential leadership, to educate them that governing is messier than campaigning and policy more of a grind than rhetoric.

Step Three: Communicate with persuadable voters. The goal here was to remind swings and independents just how bad the jobs and economic situations were at the peak of the financial crisis when Bush was leaving office.

Step Four: Road test the campaign's general election message. The Obama administration began cautiously setting forth a second-term agenda, which they planned to tweak as necessary once the GOP landed on a nominee and it became apparent which voters and counties were needed to win key states.

Step Five: Manage important political relationships. This included making sure Bernie Sanders did not undertake a nomination challenge to Obama; giving care and feeding to allies in the Democratic orbit, including labor unions and other interest groups; building field operations in the battleground states; and linking up with Democratic governors and other elected officials who would be instrumental in securing 270 electoral votes.

This plan was executed with a Spock-like efficiency that befitted the hyper-logical man for whom the reelection effort was designed.

Of course, unlike Obama, Donald Trump is in no way disciplined or methodically rational, and comparing the two is like comparing a well-rested lion with a rabbit on cocaine. But Trump's team will have made substantial progress on most of these items and more before Christmas 2019, while the eventual Democratic nominee will be far behind Trump, on the precipice of the painful primary gauntlet.

The strategists largely discount the chances of a frightful situation in which no Democrat goes to the convention with a majority or even a meaningful plurality of the delegates, and two or more competitors fight it out in Milwaukee, leaving the party in a shamble of conflict and controversy. This scenario is possible but unlikely.

The strategists agree that a far more probable outcome is that a sole Democratic candidate will have put together enough wins and delegates to be considered the presumptive nominee in March, as roughly two-thirds of the total delegates will have been allocated by the end of the month. March 3 has seventeen contests, including California, Texas, Massachusetts, Colorado, and Virginia; March 10 has six, including Michigan; and March 17 has voting in Florida, Ohio, Illinois, and Arizona. By then the leading candidate will almost certainly venture to step alone from the pack into the flush of summer.

And that will be the moment at which President Trump poses the greatest danger.

Team Trump will begin to attack the Democrat in every conceivable manner and on every available platform. TV and YouTube spots portraying the Democratic candidate as a socialist, or at least a socialist sympathizer. Targeted Facebook and search engine ads distorting liberal positions on issues such as criminal justice, health care, and immigration. Presidential Twitter rants speckled with disinformation, outrageous insults, and belittling nicknames.

From March onward, the Democrat could end up in a political no-man's land. Declared the winner by the media; attacked by Trump; left with scant campaign funds; forced to devote more time, money, and energy to the remaining contests; unable to begin a running mate search, convention planning, or general election strategizing in earnest; and lacking the open support of unions, Super PACs, a host of additional prominent groups, and the Democratic National Committee—which would almost certainly have to stay neutral after the 2016 favoritism debacle with Clinton and Sanders.

Unless the presumptive nominee has a unified party and a mathematical majority of delegates (unlikely, since even after March, there will be ten more nights of pending primaries and caucuses stretching through Puerto Rico on June 7), she or he will be exposed to attacks from nomination rivals, activists, and Republicans. Given the divisions in the Democratic Party, and the personalities and policy proposals of the leading contenders, there are any number of possibilities that might lead to prolonged discord, with runners-up scrabbling for delegates, defending their values, and attempting to claw back into nomination play. Just look at the previous two contested Democratic nomination battles. In both 2008 and 2016, the second-place candidates (Hillary Clinton in 2008 and Bernie Sanders in 2016) refused to bow to party pressure and media judgment, and continued the pursuit of the nomination long after the press and the establishment considered the result a foregone conclusion.

In 2008, Clinton lingered in the race even past the time that it became politically and mathematically impossible to overtake Barack Obama in the delegate count. In May of that year, the *Chicago Tribune* wrote, "If the 2008 Democratic presidential race were a baseball season, Hillary Clinton would need the greatest comeback in major-league history to clinch the nomination."

The Obama campaign was irked and impatient, eager to have the nomination fight in the rearview, and indignant that Hillary refused to concede. Although Obama himself instructed his team to employ a gentle touch when nudging Clinton out of the race, his advisors were impatient. They knew it was only a matter of weeks, but they also knew that every week mattered, as her continued presence kept them from fully shifting to a general election focus.

Clinton, meanwhile, was as indignant as Team Obama. She wanted to give every last voter a chance to be heard and personally guide the denouement of her historic effort to shatter what she called "that highest, hardest glass ceiling." It was not until June 2008 that she delivered her concession speech, a proud, eloquent oration in which she expressed gratitude to her supporters and respect for Obama. "I have seen his strength and determination, his grace and his grit," she said. "We may have started on separate journeys but today our paths have merged and we're all heading toward the same destination." Nevertheless, hard feelings on both sides clung through the Democratic convention that August.

One might imagine that this experience would have imbued Clinton with empathy and patience in 2016 when Bernie

Sanders chose to continue his rival campaign for the Democratic nomination into the spring and early summer. After all, Clinton was acutely familiar with the sensation of being wrangled, herded, and bullied out of a presidential race that she had entered with passion, patriotism, and precision. But instead, Clinton was once again indignant. From her perspective, Sanders had run a dishonest campaign, was afforded undeservedly glowing press coverage, had dodged deep scrutiny, and owed it to the party to unify their teams and shift the target to Trump.

But to Sanders and his devotees, the race was not over, Clinton was an unacceptable alternative, conventions (and the convention) be damned. On June 6, the Associated Press calculated that Clinton had secured the necessary delegates to win the nomination, but it was not until July 12 that Sanders released a statement endorsing her. Throughout the interminable five-week window, Clinton and her team steamed over Sanders' tenacity, calculating daily how much more difficult it was going to be to win over those increasingly staunch, angry Bernie backers whose voices were needed at the convention and whose votes were needed in November. Clinton showed little recognition that it is hard to end a hard-fought campaign that has encompassed heart and soul.

"It was not lost on some of us that it was hypocritical," says one strategist. "Hillary stayed in her race and then she got angry at Bernie for staying in his race. She knew better than anyone what it was like to come so close and have so many people counting on you and cheering you on, and then have members of your own party trying to push you out the door. But she instead was marked as a sore winner against Bernie and a sore loser against Obama, and didn't seem to have any perspective either time."

Adding to the toxic mix was the sexism at play in both of Clinton's races. When Clinton was reluctant to concede in 2008, she was often portrayed as an irrational spoiler, a shrewish nuisance, a cloying wet rag dampening the fun and mojo of

America's cool new bro, an annoying lady who had overstayed her welcome. In 2016, her frustration with Sanders was transfigured as thirsty and out-of-touch, difficult and dismaying. In the 2020 race, a record number of female candidates joined the fray, and Trump's personal and political history with women suggests what is likely to come. The strategists expect the president to push all the rusty, antiquated, anti-feminist buttons he can reach to sow unrest in the Democratic Party and stir his conservative base.

The strategists view the protracted 2008 and 2016 battles as twin cautionary tales with a single abiding message: Not this time. Undoubtedly, they say, presidential candidates should be trusted and respected enough to craft their own campaign arcs, but 2020 has special circumstances. Sacrifices must be made, not just for the party but for history. Says a strategist who has been involved in razor-sharp races, "We all get it. Candidates put their whole lives on the line, and then they are told to get out for the sake of the party. That hurts, especially in cases like last time when the party wasn't exactly fair. But we can't have a month or two of intramural unrest when we need to focus on Trump."

"Just remember the stakes," says a strategist. "This president is utterly incompetent. This is not a situation we have ever experienced before. He came into the White House knowing absolutely nothing about policy and has learned nothing. For those of us who thought he could be influenced by smart staffers, we were wrong. They can't control him. He's a joke internationally. He's not just ignorant, he's insulting. I think we all have a different idea of what the enemy looks like. John McCain, Bob Dole, Mitt Romney. They'd all be fine presidents. George H. W. Bush, 41. What I wouldn't give to have a person like that in the White House today."

"Trump is a menace," asserts one Democrat. "He's got to be stopped. I don't want to get melodramatic, but we have to think of our children. What damage can Trump do in four more years? His ego and vanity will be satisfied because he will have won two terms, but Trump as a lame duck is a really dangerous proposition. God only knows what he's capable of."

In the abstract, for a second-, third-, or fourth-place presidential candidate, staying in the ring for reasons of ideology or self-interest is not a crazy or unreasonable position. Let the voters in all the states and territories have their say, influence the party platform, help craft the message of the convention, and shape the direction and makeup of the government should the Democratic Party take back the White House. And chant the mantra that burns in the soul of every presidential hopeful—*it ain't over 'til it's over.* Under the rules of the 2020 cycle, should the frontrunner fumble and fall short of an absolute majority of delegates on the first convention ballot, the party and elected officials who are so-called superdelegates will cast votes in all subsequent rounds. The presumptive nominee is just that—*presumptive*—until the convention reaches a conclusion.

One is welcome to debate the merits of bowing out gracefully versus fighting until the end. Presidential contenders are nearly always a mix of principles, passion, ego, fragility, arrogance, idealism, and drive. But, as the strategists repeat again and again, Trump elevates the risks and the stakes. And for the likely nominee, the pressure at this moment will be unprecedented.

When Obama was navigating this stretch in 2008, it was less harrowing, even if his high command found Clinton's lingering presence to be an exasperating distraction. There was no ideological division between the two combatants, Obama was in no real danger of losing the nomination, he was not at a financial disadvantage, and there was no incumbent lying in wait. Much of the establishment closed ranks behind him while allowing Clinton to conclude her quest and make peace at the convention. In 2016, Clinton faced an ideological divide with Sanders, but the numbers were in her favor and Trump was widely dismissed as a general election threat.

For a presumptive nominee in 2020, a protracted fight would almost certainly result in pummeling from all political sides, an endless stream of process stories from the press, a struggle to focus on message or image, and campaign coffers scraped bare.

In 2008, Obama kept his public image largely intact, having vanquished two powerful candidates in Hillary Clinton and John Edwards, and electrified the media and voters with his brains, charisma, and personal story as the nation's potential first African American president. Bill Clinton, on the other hand, was so battered and bruised when he became the de facto nominee in 1992, that the *New York Times* and other leading news organizations speculated that the party establishment would wrest the nomination away from him and deliver it to another, more reliable Democratic pol.

A campaign's private money crisis will be just as worrisome as public image. Some observers insist that a financial imbalance in a presidential contest is no longer determinative, pointing to Trump's victory over Clinton despite being outspent. But Trump wrapped up his nomination battle far more quickly, while the costly Clinton-Sanders tussle dragged on. And Trump is unparalleled in his ability to garner earned media, which in a presidential race is typically more valuable than paid advertising.

With a well-funded incumbent in the race, the challenger faces even greater hardship. Most instructive is probably Obama versus Romney in 2012. In that race, Romney effectively secured the nomination in early March, but his campaign ran out of money and neither the Republican National Committee nor any outside group could match Team Obama's massive advertising spending, which lashed him for weeks. Romney was defenseless, and the assaults on his character took their toll. In 2020, the Democratic contest is hugely competitive and the collective fundraising relatively weak. At the exact moment when a fresh wave of voters begins to pay attention, the frontrunner will most assuredly be broke.

Obama was the first post-Watergate incumbent to decline to participate in the system under which a candidate accepts federal funding during the nomination season and the general election. His team made the calculated decision that it could access more through its own fundraising than it could using taxpayer money. In 2020, Trump will be the second incumbent to run for reelection with that advantage. While the Trump team has spent extensively throughout 2019, the strategists believe that it will earmark tens or even hundreds of millions of dollars to bury the Democratic candidate under an avalanche of negative TV and digital ads during this most vulnerable period. Almost none of the Democratic candidates in the race is capable of significantly self-funding a campaign.

The presumptive nominee will not be entirely without options for financial rescue—the Democratic National Committee, Super PACs, other groups, and the campaign itself can always dig around for money. But the strategists warn that this will merely expose new problems. Because of the backlash against the Democratic Party from the leftover blatant favoritism shown to Clinton by the DNC in 2016, there remains a skittishness about partiality toward any candidate. Thus fundraising or spending coordination between the apparent nominee and the DNC would be verboten. Furthermore, the committee has had fundraising struggles of its own under its chairman, Tom Perez, and does not have a bounty of cash to contribute as it is.

There is, however, plenty of money in the hands of independent groups, including Priorities USA, American Bridge, and several political operations funded by the super rich. During this cycle, they have all harnessed tens of millions of dollars and built sophisticated research and media operations in an attempt to drive up Trump's negatives. But these groups will be under the same pressure as the DNC to stay neutral. Says an advisor who has been involved with Democratic Super PACs, "This is the conundrum. You have candidates that represent constituencies in the party that are all really important. Right? So you're balancing how much can you piss them off if they're not the one that you're defending."

According to another strategist with deep experience in presidential politics and the Super PAC world, this is the stage when the presumptive nominee will have to use dexterity and diplomacy to unite the Democratic-left constellation, including labor unions, into one camp. It will require tact and skill to cajole the runners-up into halting their efforts or to flaunt a show of support so massive that the groups with funds and influence declare the race over and start spending money to defend the de facto nominee.

Of course, the relief might be short-lived as new problems arise. Trump will almost certainly repeat his 2016 refrain that the Democrats have rigged the system. And fighting back against these charges will be tough. As a manifestation of the party's move to the populist left, the major presidential candidates across the political spectrum decried Super PACs in 2019 and, breaking recent practice, refused to form their own. Justifying a sudden embrace of the world of fat cats and big-money donors in order to bicker with Team Trump will require some verbal gymnastics. And even if the groups do offer aid, it does not mean the assistance will actually be resonant or potent.

Many of the strategists refer to the Obama-Romney example to demonstrate the magnitude of the dilemma. As a cash-strapped Romney cowered beneath the onslaught of tens of millions of dollars in negative ads sent forth by the incumbent, friendly Super PACs rushed to his defense. But before long, he found that voter and media reactions to their rebuttals were tepid at best. Political science data shows what political pros have always known—positive or negative ads by outside groups simply do not have the same impact on voters as ads run by campaigns. There are a lot of wonky reasons for this, and strategists in both parties and academic researchers will be delighted to explain them. But bottom line, this kind of money could not save Romney and it cannot be counted on to save the Democratic nominee, even if well-funded allies decide to intercede. And if the nominee is on the far left and does not inspire unadulterated confidence from the mainstream groups, the problem will only be magnified.

That leaves tapping money from the campaign. Romney set the precedent of borrowing cash using funds raised for the general election as collateral, money that he could not siphon until he formally accepted the nomination at the convention. That netted him $20 million. But he also spent an inordinate amount of his valuable time going to fundraisers (a burden he would carry with him far into the general election). And if the Democrats nominate someone who has eschewed big-money, bundled checks from the traditional donor class, this labor-intensive attempt to collect funds will not even be a choice.

The strategists see a ray of hope. The Democrats have become monsters at raising money online, through email appeals and the service ActBlue, which stores a contributor's credit card data to allow for easy repeated giving. By the time there is a de facto nominee, the party might be closing in on a universe of ten million donors or more. The leading candidate will have an opportunity to solicit funds from all the Democratic donors who saw their top picks stumble and fall but who still want to contribute to the party effort.

Larry Grisolano explains how it worked for the Obama campaign in 2008 and 2012: "You can plan for a little bit. It didn't happen overnight. Somebody flips the switch, but you go out and you advertise for donors in the places where you would expect to find a lot of supporters and they click through to your webpage. We did this in the Obama campaign in 2008, but we had so much organic traffic, we were much more focused on when somebody shows up at the door, what do you do to make sure that they come in? In 2011 and 2012, we were far more focused on the outreach, to go out and draw people in. I think we got really good at it."

The Obama team used a crude but effective formula. "Our guys would calculate, okay, if somebody comes into the door today, what's the lifetime value of that donation?" says Grisolano. "So they give $25 today and we think we can get them to give another $25 six weeks later, so on and so forth. So their lifetime value is $200 or something. So we had a ratio. We were able to tell the Internet team, 'You can spend as much money as you want, as long as the return on the investment is $1 for every $2 that comes in.'"

From a practical and psychological point of view, the strategists say, it is vital that the prospective nominee make several early shows of force to demonstrate that the coffers can be replenished, and much more quickly than Romney was able to do. As in all elements of society and sociology, money and success beget money and success, and the candidate will need major mojo to impress the voters, assuage the media, invigorate donors, and send a message to the White House. One strategist suggests holding a telethon, complete with celebrities, entertainers, sports figures, and real people, some of whom would talk about why they regret their vote for Trump in 2016.

Money can buy neither happiness nor elections. Raising sufficient funds at this juncture is only the first piece. A campaign must plan its TV and digital ad buys and it cannot move on that venture until it knows how much it can spend. But there is no rational, clean way to budget when the effectiveness of the fundraising effort is an hour-by-hour proposition. Therefore, a campaign must empower its digital and fundraising teams to work together to maximize how much can be brought in each day and predict how much to expect in the longer term.

Once the money flow is under control, the actual work begins. The presumptive nominee needs to make certain that the state parties in the targeted battlegrounds are on track to lay the foundation for field activity that can match the operations set in place by the competition. The RNC and the White House reelection campaign will have been designing and administering their plan, with ample resources, for months. These are the "coordinated campaigns," the partnerships between the nominee's team and the state parties, which so fixated Paul Tully.

"They need to have a plan [for] the coordinated campaign," says Craig Smith. "So when that day happens, they already have the infrastructure built to efficiently spend the money that will be there. So they don't have to kind of build the car while they are driving it."

The strategists say the campaign needs to do a thorough analysis of the key state party operations, and those that are found wanting must get a change in direction and leadership. The strategists were optimistic that the DNC and state parties will be eager to accept guidance from the winning campaign and relieved to sync up and unite both the field agencies and the party more broadly, once a sole candidate has an iron grip on a majority of the delegates or all the other candidates surrender.

It is at this point, the strategists recommend, that the candidate pivot in full to a general election message. Any positions taken in the nomination season, as well as potentially controversial past statements, videos, or votes that have not yet surfaced, must be comprehensively evaluated. All these elements will be viewed in the fresh context of the general election, especially with Trump as an opponent. And it is critical to remember that virtually everything is unearthed during a general. Usually. Eventually. George W. Bush, the son of a president, made it through two and a half decades, two gubernatorial races and victories, and most of a presidential campaign before it was revealed, on November 2, 2000, mere days before the election, that he was arrested in 1976 for drunk driving, his teenage sister, Doro, a passenger in the car.

Once this mess of money and reputation and allies and frenemies has been sorted, it is time, say the strategists, for the candidate to steal a moment to recharge. The Democrat who makes it through the primary contest will have endured an utterly draining, stressful extended period, and things are only just starting to heat up.

Whichever candidate withstands the rigors of the nomination ordeal will doubtlessly be exhausted at the end of the process, but even rest must be meted out judiciously. The candidate has to reorient the team for the general election, prepare to command the Democratic Party apparatus, raise still more money, incorporate family members more intricately into the campaign, contemplate convention planning, train for the fall debates, and conceive of a budget and strategy that can carry her or him all the way to November. But none of this can be done properly if the nominee is too tired or burned out to think clearly. Help, however, is on the horizon.

Brace yourself: it's time to choose a running mate.

CHAPTER EIGHT
VEEPSTAKES UPENDED

LESSON: THE SELECTION
PROCESS SHOULD BE QUIET,
THE CHOICE ON-MESSAGE.

After all those months of speculation and predictions and horse-race number-crunching about which candidate will ultimately snag the nomination, one might imagine that, with a Democratic challenger finally in place, the political-media world will take a moment for quiet reflection, contemplation, meditation. Ha ha ha. Within the blink of an eye, the press and social media will move on to natter about who the newly minted leader will select as a running mate. Who will be a heartbeat away? How will the nominee balance gender, ethnicity, age, geography, ideology? Will the choice appease underrepresented factions of the electorate or be more conventional? Will the mates like and trust each other? Will they make a pretty picture? Will there be good chemistry? How will the spouses interact? Will the pick perform well against Mike Pence? What nickname will Trump apply, and how nasty and evocative will it be?

Veepstakes inevitably sparks pure mania in the politico-media world, a quadrennial journalistic competition in which there is no clear winner but most assuredly clear losers—the

American people and the candidates, who would be better off talking about their plans for the country than the latest incremental developments in their running-mate search.

My own history scheming to break veepstakes picks each cycle is not particularly inspirational. In 1992, when I was a reporter assigned to cover the Clinton campaign, I chased the story like a relentless puppy, chewing on my share of scooplets as Bill Clinton deliberated over his choice. This was the pre-smartphone, pre–social media era; journalists still recorded on videotape, printed their newsbreaks in the next day's paper, and received confidential info from whispered asides and covert tête-à-têtes rather than by texts. My mobile phone was housed in a valise the size of a football.

My life in July 1992 was a blur of legwork, hustle, Sherlock Holmesian detecting, and nagging, some of which paid off. My colleagues and I captured exclusive video of a beleaguered and slightly annoyed Bob Kerrey, as the contender raced through the lobby of a Little Rock Holiday Inn Express in a vain attempt to escape from me and the camera crew after he met surreptitiously with Clinton at the Arkansas governor's mansion. I reported on another previously undisclosed Clinton meeting, this one with Florida senator Bob Graham. I got wind of last-minute campaign polling that tested the relative benefits of adding Al Gore or Mario Cuomo to the ticket. I worked around the clock for days, until, exhausted, I slept through the post-midnight ringing of my hotel room telephone, missing the call from a high-level Clinton campaign source who had decided to give me the scoop on Al Gore. By the time I woke up, bleary and befuddled, another news organization had the story.

In 1996, I helped deploy veep-seeking teams all over the country, assigning reporters to tail every possible prospect we believed to be under Bob Dole's consideration. None of the half-dozen hopefuls we tracked included Dole's actual pick,

Jack Kemp, the former NFL quarterback, Buffalo-area congressman, and cabinet secretary. I continued to work my sources until I had the goods on Kemp, and stewed when my news colleagues instead credited legendary columnist Bob Novak with the reveal that Dole had settled on Kemp. When I subsequently reported definitively that Dole had offered the slot to Kemp and that Kemp had officially accepted, no one noticed or cared.

I was on double duty in 2000, digging for veepstakes data on both the Al Gore and George W. Bush campaigns. Walking toward home in New York City one summer evening after a long day on the case, I came upon a large law enforcement presence and a throng of gawkers surrounding the building across the street from my apartment. I ascertained that Gore was inside, attending a fundraiser. Mostly as a joke, I contacted one of his traveling aides and suggested that if the vice president wanted to stop over at my place after his event, I could offer him a beer.

Fifteen minutes later, a team of stone-faced Secret Service agents were at my door, looking to sweep the place. Gore and a few staffers followed soon after. The vice president and I drank Heinekens and chatted almost exclusively about veepstakes. Gore was poker-faced. He asked me whom I thought he would pick, and I guessed Missouri congressman Dick Gephardt. He asked me why, and I explained my reasoning. Gore listened pleasantly, finished his beer, thanked me graciously for my hospitality, and took his leave. The words "Joe Lieberman" were never uttered by either of us during his visit, and I did not come close to breaking either that story or Bush's drafting of Dick Cheney.

In 2008, Barack Obama's selection of Joe Biden happened in slow motion, practically in public, so there was little tension or competition among my peers. But John McCain's pick was a veepstakes classic. It was a badly kept secret that the Arizona

Republican was longing to tap Lieberman, his Democratic colleague and buddy, for the position. When McCain's campaign staff and Republican allies forbade him from reaching across the aisle to make his favored pick, he settled on the maverick choice of Alaska governor Sarah Palin.

I was caught off guard when Governor Palin emerged as McCain's surprise decision, but I happened to be on live television when the word leaked out. After wasting a few minutes on zealous efforts to track private planes leaving Alaska, I settled down enough to participate in a conversation about Sarah Palin's prospects as McCain's running mate. Unlike most of the political reporters covering the story, I had actually met the governor. I happened to be in Alaska on vacation in August 2006, two years earlier, arriving the night Palin won the Republican gubernatorial nomination. I spent my holiday touring the glories of the Alaskan landscape and learning about the up-and-coming former Wasilla mayor, a compelling, resourceful, do-it-all mother of four (by 2008, a mother of five). I eventually met Palin by chance at the state fair in Palmer, and had a lovely conversation with her and her husband, Todd. She was quick, bright, enthusiastic, and impressive, and our casual fifteen-minute exchange at the fair, surrounded by green mountains and cobalt sky, made me, for a fleeting moment, one of national journalism's leading experts on Sarah Palin the morning her selection was revealed.

In 2016, I was one of two reporters, along with Vaughn Hillyard of NBC News, staking out Governor Mike Pence's residence in a quiet Indianapolis neighborhood, believing that he was the frontrunner to be added to the Republican ticket. Sure enough, Donald Trump and members of his family, including Jared Kushner and Ivanka Trump, pulled up in their motorcade for an unannounced, clandestine meeting with Governor Pence. My journalist's tools had evolved over the past two and a half decades; no more football phones or sheaves of wrinkled faxes or notes handwritten on alehouse paper napkins. But now I was faced with a 21st-century reportorial dilemma. Should I tweet the fact that Trump was at the residence (thereby achieving an incremental newsbreak) or stay quiet and hope for more details before other reporters got wind of the conclave? I decided to tweet, then watched with amusement as local, national, and international news media descended on the scene, first a few, then a dozen, then swarms, temporarily turning the peaceful perimeter of the Pence household into the Midwest equivalent of Trump Tower, with all the drama, lights, and chaos of 57th Street and Fifth Avenue at Christmas.

Depending on timing and how the campaign handles the selection process, the veepstakes story line can dominate the news for weeks. The strategists have all sorts of ideas about what the candidate should and should not do when making the selection. But foremost, they are adamant that the campaign not allow the veepstakes sweepstakes to become the long-running, all-consuming narrative it has been in the past.

The reason is, once again, clear. Beating Trump requires the Democratic nominee to drive a core message every day. "We have had a twenty-two-whatever-plus-person primary and we need to focus the game," says Jill Alper. "We need to get right down to, 'what's the argument?' You know, the two people making the argument." When all the chatter is absorbed by idle conjecture about who will be picked for the number two slot—i.e., endless debates over every possible name from every possible faction with every possible resume, all of which become absolutely meaningless once the choice is made—no room is left for discussion of health-care reform or the downsides of the Trump economy. Valuable pre-convention days are wasted, with little opportunity for the candidate to charm the electorate or burnish the only brand that really matters.

Meanwhile, the veepstakes story line drags on and on. Members of the media often seem to enjoy nothing more than listening to their own speculation and opinions, so pontificating about the best possible vice presidential choice is a temptation, especially if the alternative topics involve actual policy. And the organic conclusion from a drawn-out selection process is that the nominee is having trouble making up his or her mind about whom to choose. A real-time narrative about a potential president being unable to reach a conclusion on an important matter projects weakness, not strength.

Why, then, has every nominee from both parties allowed the process to spiral out of control, overwhelming every other message the campaign wants to push? The strategists cite several reasons. Most presidential nominees emerge from the primary battlefield shell-shocked and chastened, coping with the lingering frustrations of months of unfamiliar impotence and an inability to control the news cycle. (Most, not all. Not Trump. *No, sir-ee.*) Because of the media's utter and utterly irrational obsession with veepstakes, many nominees find the sudden power intoxicating, a balm after so many slights and dings and indignities, so many disparaging opinion pieces and withering cable news asides.

"God, they hear so much negative stuff all year," exclaims one strategist. "It can be so gratuitous. It can feel personal. Or, they do all this good stuff and get ignored. They are always so surprised by all the negativity. Running for president is hard, you know?" All of a sudden, the nominee alone is the keeper of information everyone in the business of politics wants. She or he merely can nudge an advisor to float a new name to a friendly reporter, or suggest whom some finalists might be, and the hungry press pack will pounce upon the morsel, rolling it around like a sheet of taffy in a bag of nuts. The impression of control can be an exhilarating experience for a politician.

Yet that sensation is misapplied. The nominee might imagine that she or he is dictating the conversation, but every element of the campaign is ineluctably distilled into this one issue during this period. Questions of policy, judgment, and agenda become about the running mate, with all stories, tweets, and television coverage reflected through this prism.

Democratic presidential candidates have an additional, particular motivation for the slow veep striptease. The campaign imagines it can appease various interest groups and constituencies and, more recently, social media, by leaking out a rainbow coalition of diverse prospects allegedly under serious consideration. This never works. With the exception of Walter Mondale in 1984, no Democratic presidential candidate has ever picked anyone but a white man with whom to run, and the stakeholders who longed for diversity were disappointed every time. The strategists say the process of floating names and then dashing hopes has done more harm than good. "They think you can curry favor with certain constituencies," says John Sasso. "You know, 'I gotta have an African American. I gotta have a woman.' It doesn't do you any good if you're not going to pick them at the end. So just make the pick."

Campaigns also float names as trial balloons, to see what the reaction is like, a common practice in industries from manufacturing to moviemaking. In the olden days of presidential elections, feedback would come from the elite, establishment universe of three television networks, two national weekly news magazines, a handful of national newspapers, and the various wire services. Back then, such testing of the waters probably made sense.

In today's world, however, the strategists say there is such a glut of instant feedback and criticism, often without any real knowledge of the person or their positions, that the experiment can be distorted and rendered pointless. Not just pointless but needlessly detrimental. A perfectly solid choice might be subjected to quick-and-dirty investigative reporting and attempts from various quarters to throw some mud for sport, competition, or mischief. And nothing gives Twitter users more joy than trashing someone they have never met, and know little about. The campaign might be denied an accurate, real-world assessment and the veep candidate unfairly tainted.

"I think that a lot of people have made this mistake," says Sasso. "I would try to do it quietly. Of course, there will be some speculation. You can't avoid that. But I would keep it as quiet as you can until you're ready to make the announcement. And then hopefully that person would reinforce your own qualities and your own attributes, and your own view of how to run the country. Ride that for whatever period of time you can."

Prolonging the process also attracts pests, much like leaving some freshly sliced honeydew out on the back porch. During the run-up to the selection, reporters will pass all their waking hours trying to get the scoop. They will look for clues in every conceivable place, calling sign-printing companies, tracking airplane tail numbers, snooping into the whereabouts of friends, relatives, and children. But political journalists will spend most of their time relentlessly calling the nominee's advisors and begging for names. Who is on the shortlist? The long list? The finalist list? If they can't get names, they will plead for hints and clues. These calls, texts, instant messages, and emails are so incessant that they become a fanatical preoccupation.

Campaign aides try to ignore these entreaties as best they can, but, the strategists say, the volume of incoming is so high that it produces an unavoidable distraction for the staffers who are at their busiest, with serious work to be done on convention planning, fundraising, debate preparation, and defensive maneuvers against the opposition. Furthermore, these staffers usually have little to do with the selection process itself. "It sounds harmless, in a silly sort of way," says one advisor, "but it's really a problem. It eats up a lot of time and puts a strain on relationships with the reporters you need to get along with, because you either have to dodge them or you don't give them what they want."

There is nothing a campaign can do to make the media's veepstakes obsession disappear, say the operatives. Names will leak out from other sources, including the cohorts of those under consideration and those whom the campaign contacts for input. But the strategists believe the fever can be tamped down significantly if the campaign is firm about not playing the game. They recommend that the candidate be absolutely disciplined with the press and, when necessary, with the staff, repeating a strict message to all media queries: *I am working hard every day to beat Donald Trump by talking about my plans for America's families; when, after a meticulous, careful, and confidential process, I have figured out who the best possible running mate is to serve with me in the White House, I will announce it.* The strategists say exerting such discipline could buy any number of weeks for the candidate, giving the campaign a chance to shape a message of strength and purpose each day.

It should be noted that this assessment of press behavior is purely factual, described at length by more than a dozen strategists who have dealt with it firsthand. But the media's fascination with the more glamorous, diverting, or titillating aspects of a campaign is understandable. It is borne from valuable components of human nature, such as curiosity, diligence, and a healthy competitive spirit. Just because it is also colored by some of the baser instincts as well—pettiness, swagger, insecurity, and rivalry—does not diminish it.

After the nominee has pledged to use diligence, he or she should make a few essential decisions. First, pick the right person—not the running mate just yet but a qualified, stolid, and trustworthy advisor who can take charge of the selection process. The strategists recommend appointing an attorney with access to the resources of a large law firm. This person should have a political background as well. He or she must have appropriate previous experience, be completely discreet, show total loyalty to the presidential candidate, and not be afraid to speak the truth.

The strategists all agree that Team Trump will launch an unprecedented, multi-platform attack on the credentials, record, and political strengths of the person who is chosen as the running mate. So the vet, the choice, and the launch all have to be rock solid.

Proper vetting will require a team to carry out the background check (finances, legal issues, past relationships), and also a two-part political test. What exists in a person's previous record that could be controversial? Does he or she possess the political skills necessary to campaign and debate on the national stage? A small group of the candidate's advisors will consult on these questions, but the initial research and confidential interviews must be completed first by the designated team to prepare the evaluations.

Then, at some point, the candidate needs to have face-to-face meetings with the finalists. "That's a tricky one," says a strategist. "The meetings themselves can be awkward, because the tone has to be just right. These are two people who need to work together and be judged in the highest-stakes way, and they may be total strangers or even have bad blood. And you have to keep it all secret from the press." It takes a lot of planning, the strategists say, to pull off these discussions without the media finding out about them. Nothing sets journalists' hair on fire more than the chase to capture details of the meetings or, better, video of the presumptive nominee and potential running mate in the same frame.

When it comes time to make the selection from the final shortlist, the strategists agree on a series of guidelines. "There's no such thing as a perfect pick," says one. "You are never going to be able to tick every box with one person. Also, you want chemistry between the two, but you have to remember that almost anyone in the running for vice president really wants to be president. There's always going to be that tension. So it's best to try to focus on who can help you win, and worry about the other dynamics later. That's tough to do." It is best, therefore, to keep the requirements uncomplicated and straightforward.

First, do no harm. If an applicant has anything at all in his or her background that gives the chief vetter concern about risking significant controversy, move on. Second, get some real mileage out of the running mate. The campaign should determine, with polling and other research, which selection can actually help draw votes in a battleground state, improve the candidate's standing with key voting groups, or amplify the brand. As Bob Shrum puts it, don't make a "complacent" pick. Choose someone who will help you win. And most important, select a mate who the press and the electorate will look at and say without reservation or hesitation, *This person is ready to be president from Day One*. It is the simplest and most important part of the entire veepstakes process.

Yet despite these guidelines, the campaign should never forget that the selection process is not about the running mate, no matter how attractive or carefully chosen. It is about the nominee. For voters and the media, the whole point of the process is to observe how the nominee makes the first and most important major decision in the national spotlight. If the candidate shows responsibility and judgment, and meets the "one heartbeat away" standard, the test has been passed.

Once the running mate decision is made in private, the strategists suggest keeping pesky reporters at bay long enough to plan the announcement carefully, with a big reveal at a place and time of the campaign's choosing. This will allow the event to be crafted and choreographed so the duo can present a united front, the country can feel positive about the choice, the campaign can maximize the resulting burst of online fundraising, and the remarks can highlight the team spirit, punch the campaign's core message, and blast President Trump.

After the announcement, say several strategists, break from the recent tradition of "tick-tock" briefings, in which a giddy staff recounts to reporters the exhaustive chronology of the process, complete with cloak-and-dagger anecdotes, the names of all the finalists, the cunning skullduggery, the roads not traveled. "Don't play that game," advises a strategist. "Let your choice speak for itself and move forward."

If, of course, the Democrats end up with a contested convention, and the nominee is not determined until July, some of this advice is irrelevant and can be tossed right out the window. If two or more candidates head to Milwaukee with enough delegates to stake a claim for the nomination, the strategists believe that at least one of them will announce a prospective running mate before or at the convention in order to win over additional delegates and endorsements.

Under this scenario, the Democrats potentially could face a disaster like the one in 1972, when George McGovern was forced to make his pick on the fly at the convention itself, and ended up with an unvetted Thomas Eagleton on the ticket, a choice that was withdrawn after the Missouri senator's past treatments for depression became public. "If there's no nominee," says a Democratic strategist, "it's going to be crazy. But the candidates still in the race have to come to the convention with a list of options. Fully vetted options, no matter how busy they are. We can't let this become chaos." Raw political considerations may not allow the eventual nominee to tap a first choice, but the party cannot withstand a selection that implodes, with Trump and his allies ready to strike.

One strategist suggests that the drama of a contested convention could be turned into a boon if two of the leading contenders form a unity ticket. "There's actually a likelihood that one of the candidates running does not win and becomes the

VP nominee," the strategist says. "So I think major signals can be sent to say 'there's an inclusive united front against Donald Trump, and the Democrats are more united than they have been in years going into the general election.'" And what better way to conclude a convention, to turn chaos into comity?

CHAPTER NINE
ON WISCONSIN

LESSON: THE NATIONAL CONVENTION
HAS TO DEFINE AND UNITE.

"Hell no, DNC, we won't vote for Hillary!"
"Hell no, DNC, we won't vote for Hillary!"
"HELL NO, DNC, WE WON'T VOTE FOR HILLARY!"

On July 25, 2016, the first day of the Democratic National Convention, Franklin Delano Roosevelt Park in South Philadelphia was echoing with the chants of angry protestors. The Wells Fargo Center, just across South Broad Street, was hosting the convention, and its perimeter was teaming with demonstrations. But these dissidents, a band of Bernie Sanders supporters, had the loudest voices and drew media coverage like oxygen to a red-hot flame.

Bernie backers had come from all over the United States, numbering in the thousands, to oppose a Clinton nomination and disrupt the proceedings. Most of the Sandernistas had no official connection to the convention but had set up encampments across Philadelphia to hunker down for the week. They were there to be seen, to be heard, to vent their anger—not at Donald Trump but at Hillary Clinton, the person whom they felt had stolen the prize. "A crime has taken place, and we want the whole world to know it," said one woman who had driven up from Baltimore. They marched, sang, and called for justice. To the Clinton team, those cries of "Hell no, DNC" were as chilling as "Lock her up."

It was a sweltering day—the whole week would be stifling—but the boiling heat only matched the protesters' mood, lending a primal, earthy feel to their rage.

Laurie Cestnick, the founder of a group called Occupy DNC, had come from Waltham, Massachusetts. "We believe the process has been rigged," she said matter-of-factly. "It's kind of obvious. There are lawsuits pending, of course." The allegations were serious, and the list of culprits broad. "Racketeering charges," Cestnick clarified, "which include Hillary Clinton, the Democratic Party, certain elite people. And also media. CNN and MSNBC are also in this racketeering lawsuit. Where they came together pretty much to shut Bernie out. I mean it's pretty obvious. In recent days, people saw emails alluding to that fact, that that's pretty much what they had planned. That's no surprise to us. This is how we have been thinking for a very long time. It is surprising to people who have not been following this, or maybe Republicans who weren't that interested. But to us, it's been obvious." Cestnick enumerated some of the specific charges of tampering and interference. "We are here to be heard," she concluded gravely, "because we are mad."

Three days earlier, on July 22, the Friday before the convention got underway and the very day Clinton unveiled Virginia senator Tim Kaine as her running mate, WikiLeaks published a large trove of hacked emails from Democratic National Committee officials. They starkly revealed the patent favoritism toward Clinton's candidacy that Sanders and his backers had long suspected. Amid the howls of outrage and pressure on the party, DNC chairwoman Debbie Wasserman Schultz and several members of her senior staff were forced to resign just hours before the Wells Fargo Convention Center opened its doors, and the mood inside the hall when the proceedings began was dark, fractured, and choleric.

Clinton and Sanders had never experienced a personal rapprochement at the close of their bitter battle. Throughout their spirited duel for the nomination, Clinton had remained starchy and suspicious, while Sanders was his typical prickly self. Jane Sanders, the senator's wife, was known to hold a particularly jaundiced view of her husband's rival, which influenced how the campaign reacted to both overtures and sleights. When Sanders eventually endorsed Clinton on July 12, at a joint rally in Portsmouth, New Hampshire, their interactions were stiff, their smiles forced, and their rhetoric formulaic. Sanders supporters attended the event only to hiss and hold up signs reading "Won't Vote Hillary." Clinton's team looked on in horror.

The Clinton campaign anticipated the frost would thaw once all the Democrats convened in Philadelphia, and the nearly thirteen million people who had cast ballots for the Vermont senator during the nomination season would fall in line, especially given the looming threat of Trump. But the Clintonites underestimated the disappointment and disillusionment of the Sanders voters. And after the clashes over the party platform and the WikiLeaks release of the DNC emails, for this ardent mass of adherents, any thought of party loyalty evaporated and the notion of unity became anathema. Senior members of the Sanders team worked with the Clinton camp to instill some peace, but the passions had been unleashed.

Over in Franklin Delano Roosevelt Park, Dixie Stephens of Murfreesboro, Tennessee, sat on the ground, American flag bandana on her head, "NEVER HILLARY" sign in her hand. When asked to explain why she would not support Clinton over Trump, she was incensed. "Because she's not my candidate of choice. She's in this for herself and the one percent.

Bernie Sanders is in it for Americans, all Americans. So we're fighting the corruption from the DNC. I came all the way from Tennessee to let them know I am not happy with the corruption and election fraud that just happened."

Paul Jaeger from Parma, Michigan, was equally indignant: "The way that the process went really rubbed me the wrong way. The irregularities, starting from the beginning. I think that Hillary wasn't prepared to have an honest campaign."

Outside the convention hall, Sanders addressed a large group of his supporters and made an effort to allay their concerns and help the party move forward. "We have got to elect Hillary Clinton and Tim Kaine," he told them. In response, he was met with boos, hisses, and cries of "*No*" from his own people.

The first few days of the convention were shaded by this unrest, driving the Clinton team and the organizers to distraction. Sanders heightened the tenor of his pleas, giving a speech inside the hall and sending a text message to his supporters. "I ask you as a personal courtesy to me," he wrote, "to not engage in any kind of protest on the floor. It's of utmost importance you explain this to your delegates."

The hot tempers began to cool. While there continued to be some disruptions within the Wells Fargo Center, the Clinton and Sanders whip operations worked together to minimize the impact on the television coverage. Although the failure to bring many of Sanders' backers on board to vote for Clinton would be costly in November, Hillary was at least able to salvage her convention. By the midway point, Clinton and her team were firmly in control of the message coming out of Philadelphia, and managed to put on an exceptionally good show.

•　　•　　•

Convention planning begins several years before the election year, arranged and executed by the national committee and its staff until the presumptive nominee takes over all but the basic logistical aspects of the proceedings. Even the most organized campaign scrambles to put together a program, a platform, a surrogate operation, and all the general election planning meetings that go on behind the scenes. If the Democrats have no clear, acknowledged nominee coming into Milwaukee, the 2020 convention will see exponentially more chaos than the Clinton-Sanders mess.

And should the party nominate an establishment candidate on the first ballot, or on the second ballot with decisive backing from the superdelegates, drawn from the ranks of elected officials and party bosses, the dissension could be particularly acute.

The strategists say there are far too many variables to properly assess a contested convention. Who will the contending candidates be, and how many delegates will each of them have? How many ballots will it take for someone to reach a majority? Will the process be considered fair? How much hostility will there be from foiled supporters? How will the vice presidential pick be made? Will there be a unity ticket? Will the party be able to project any other message besides one of discord, or to do any other business at the convention?

But even if the Democrats avoid the political and logistical mayhem of a contested convention, the strategists say it is still imperative in 2020 for the party to curb the acrimony, promote harmony, and deliver their general election messages to a wide audience. Obama and Clinton were able to present a unified front in 2008 after their caustic clash, and Clinton and Sanders did their best, although the strategists say the Democrats will have to do still better in 2020. Otherwise, as before, a sizable chunk of the party's constituents will remain embittered and unenthusiastic, and will decline to go to the polls in November to back the Democrat.

The experts repeat over and over that Democratic activists and voters cannot be complacent, cannot assume that, because they find Trump to be loathsome, he will definitely lose. "I hear it all the time," says one strategist. "People think that of course the Democrats will be forced to rally around whoever ultimately gets the nomination, because it's got to be better than Trump. But that's not the way this party works or has ever worked. Our voters don't like to be bullied or told what to do." That said, the strategists uniformly hope that a strong desire to beat Trump will indeed serve as a natural adhesive for voters throughout the progressive movement.

The convention goals, the experts say, should mirror the goals of the entire campaign. From Monday, July 13 to Thursday, July 16, the Democrats must focus cleanly on energizing the base while reaching out to persuadable voters; telling the heroic life story of the nominee and highlighting the policy proposals that speak to the candidate's values; indicting the record and morals of the incumbent, while tying Trump's personal deficiencies directly to his policy failings, especially on the economy; and polishing the brand of the Democratic Party to help candidates up and down the ballot. Says Jim Margolis, who worked on the Obama and Clinton conventions and is an advisor to Senator Kamala Harris, "The broad objectives of the 2020 convention are going to be pretty similar to those of the 2016 convention. The first thing you try to do is unify the party—get everybody on board. The second thing you try to do is make sure your base is excited. And the third thing you try to do is begin the process of connecting with those voters who are still in the process of making up their mind—you want them to say, 'Okay, I'm interested and I'm going to take a look. Maybe this is someone I can get behind.' And that means you need to have programming and speakers who appeal both to our base and to independent voters. For example, in 2016, we not only featured 'Mothers of the Movement,' who lost children to gun violence, but we also showcased police chiefs who lost officers. There was a unifying dimension to that. Those elements are going to be important again."

"The difference is, people have now experienced what four years of Donald Trump is like," Margolis continues. "And a lot of the things we talked about in '16 that might have seemed over the top or alarmist have now actually happened. The campaign is going to be amped up more than previous years because people have seen what this administration is doing—we have a president who lies without hesitation, demeans people, divides, and has challenged the fundamental values of the nation. That's disconcerting to people, and our voters are going to be more motivated to come together than in '16 when they thought Hillary had the election in the bag."

The nominee will have to personally expend as much energy and effort as necessary to repair any fractures resulting from the primary fight. "This can't be farmed out," says one operative. "People who really cared about a [losing] candidate are still licking their wounds, and getting impersonal emails about unity, or hearing surrogates talk about how great the party is won't cut it. It has to come from the nominee."

That said, the strategists all agree there are two very prominent exceptions: Barack and Michelle Obama. The former first couple is expected to appear in Milwaukee and deliver unity speeches calling on Democrats to put aside differences and come together to support the ticket, and to encourage all Americans to make Donald Trump a one-term president. The powerhouse appeal and unifying magic of the Obamas are unparalleled and irreplaceable, and will go a long way toward healing party rifts.

Several strategists said it would be smart to also find a role for Bill and Hillary Clinton, although one that does not allow them to speak from the podium in prime time. While the Clintons are still popular with segments of the party, they are no longer unifying figures by any definition, even apart from the Sanders debacle. Some believe that Hillary, secretive, remote, and overconfident, bungled 2016, with her email server conflict and tone-deaf attitude toward the Clinton Foundation and her lucrative speeches. Some are reexamining Bill's personal history, never acceptable by any standard of society, through the prism of the #MeToo movement. Some feel both are representative of the past, a time in the party's history that Democrats on the left want to move beyond.

It is assumed that there will be a speaking slot for most, if not all, of the two dozen women and men who entered the 2020 nomination race. One strategist argues that these remarks should be coordinated to highlight the best each competitor has to offer, to make the whole greater than the sum of its parts. The strategist also advises that these speeches be kept short, except for those who finished near the top of the heap.

And, as it is a Democratic convention, there will indeed be plenty of celebrities—actors and comedians and music industry idols, looking great, speaking with heart and expert projection, and rocking the arena with song and dance. A strategist who has worked on several past convention programs recommends that the campaign invite a country artist for every R&B performer and a professional athlete for every Hollywood star.

The experts also have ideas for the "real people" who are trotted out every four years to show the party is empathetic, accessible, and compassionate, or to relate a positive personal story about the candidate, or a negative experience with the opposition. One strategist who worked on the 2016 convention suggests that, in 2020, the party take special steps to find speakers who have both charisma and a compelling hero story of their own. If the campaign has been able, as recommended, to recruit so-called characters beginning in the winter, the standouts can be tapped to participate at the convention and be introduced to the wider national audience from the Milwaukee stage. "Ideally," says an advisor, "you find some well-spoken Trump voters who can testify that his policies have made their lives worse."

A number of strategists praise the Clinton campaign for presenting the Democratic brand as one that encompasses the whole country—blue-collar workers, single mothers, Midwestern lawyers, Texan college students, Rust Belt pastors—not just atheists, academics, and coastal elites. "Clinton did an amazing job to recast what it means to be a patriot," says Jennifer Granholm. "The American flag was flown everywhere at that convention. And a kid in a Mariachi outfit sang 'God Bless America.' It was this notion that we are all so proud to be part of what is uniquely American, this inclusive country. And so, to me, replicating that raw patriotism because of our diversity gives a contrast with what the Republicans are doing and makes Democrats feel enormously proud. People felt so patriotic at that Democratic convention. I think that was the brilliant move. And it needs to be replicated."

It also should be taken a step further, says Charlie Baker, as a direct reproach to the president. "I would want to show the diversity of the coalition aimed against Trump," he says. "I would not go crazy, but I would want to see some military personnel. Some diversity that people would not expect. I definitely want to see some Republicans. I might want to see some Christian leaders. But I would not play down the base."

Tad Devine encourages the campaign to study, long before the convention begins, what message might be required to convince a 2016 Trump voter to switch to the Democrat. "It is really important to do some in-depth research on these people who voted for Trump, who may be available to swing this time. You have got to find out really what is motivating them to stay with him. And, most importantly, what would get people off of him. You have got to spend some time with these people and find out, what is it about him that would essentially disqualify him from being president."

Anita Dunn adds that it is rarely automatic for voters to switch to a new candidate, even if they feel disappointment with the leader they chose before. The Democrats must "help build the permission structure for people to change their votes from 2016. Because getting people to say, 'I'm not going to vote for him again' [is hard]. It is not that easy for people to admit that they've made a mistake. You have to start laying the groundwork with your convention to give people that permission structure to go change their position on someone and on a pretty big issue."

And all these messages—of patriotism, of inclusiveness, of dissatisfaction with the incumbent, of genuine promise and energy and optimism for the future—all have to be reinforced and distilled for the nominee's acceptance speech, and then infused with poetry.

Bob Shrum says, "You really have to think about the acceptance speech. You have got to make sure that it is pitched in a way that is going to lay out a general election message that is really going to matter. It has to be a strategic document. Even in this atomized media environment, that is your best chance at unmediated communication with the largest number of Americans. So you really have to focus on that. People need to feel reassured that you are up to the job of being commander-in-chief. That is sort of the baseline. But the biggest thing you have got to do is put a message out there that resonates with people at both an emotional and substantive level."

Shrum reiterates one of the most instrumental elements of a successful campaign and one of the most important pieces of advice in this book. "You cannot become a new person," he says. "You have got to build on what you have done before, but you have to build in a way that reaches out. You have to have a message that emphasizes social justice and economic justice." A strong candidate will have entered the race with a philosophy and a message that stays consistent through winter, spring, and summer. The nomination acceptance speech delivered on the night of Thursday, July 16, 2020, should be fundamentally the same in spirit and substance as the ones that were made in early 2019.

John Sasso stresses that it is imperative the candidate fully understands that a high percentage of people watching the acceptance speech live, or hearing news reports about it, will be meeting the nominee for the first time. Yes, by this point, many voters will be able to engage in an entree-length dinner-party conversation about the nominee, and a few might even be able to pen a comprehensive essay or Wikipedia entry. A majority of citizens will at least know the nominee's name and face, and probably a two-sentence resume. But the number of actual voters who have truly listened to the nominee's voice, or watched her or him gesticulate expressively, or processed the deeper rationale and agenda of the presidential bid, is always comparatively small until the convention.

"Many candidates forget that," Sasso says, noting that advisors need to push back and remind the candidate that "millions of people are going to be for the first time leaning in because they have to make a decision."

So that takes care of the poetry and prose on the main stage, but the campaign cannot forget about the scut work behind the scenes.

Ben LaBolt believes it is well overdue for the party and the campaign to modernize the PR approach to the convention. For decades the focus has been on producing palatable pictures for four nights of television coverage, and it is time, says LaBolt, to place an equal importance on the platforms where people actually get their news, customizing images and packages for different forms of media.

"The convention is currently still set up for network and cable television," LaBolt says. "But we're living in an era where most people consume information on their mobile devices. It is up to the Democratic campaign, that has to reach younger voters, to figure out how to chop up the most important pieces of bite-size content and replay those moments in front of persuadable voters or sporadic voters in the weeks to come [after the convention]. Because even though they're going to have a big TV audience, that's not enough to reach the voters that we need to reach. And I think [instead of] just a sloppy YouTube cut—the way we have run campaigns in the past—we need to do something more sophisticated this time around."

Elegant, emotional mini-movies, well-edited nuggets, charmingly raw or candid clips, and clever memes can go viral, continuing to echo all the way through the fall, offering a reminder of the best of the candidate and the message, and sustaining the brand through debate gaffes and autumn surprises.

"We have treated the conventions like the Grammys or the Oscars," says LaBolt, "where it's just this made-for-TV moment, and we've had made-for-TV moments in politics since the events in the 1960s and it is time to become more creative and more targeted about how the conventions unfold. I think there should be a much richer multimedia component, especially because the networks have been airing less and less of them. And finding a millennial who watches network television at all is pretty difficult these days. So we need to be much more creative about that. I think [some programming] should happen exclusively on digital channels, through digital outlets, through content produced directly by the campaign. We want to treat this as more than a four-day television event, and extend the reach and frequency of the event so that, over a week or two, the persuadable electorate and the electorate we need to vote, who maybe did not show up last time, gets the message going into the general election, and gets it months before Election Day, so we can continue to hammer it home on the trail."

The convention is also a good opportunity to get practical, unglamorous campaign business done. Milwaukee will be the last place where all the stakeholders will be together face-to-face, and the candidate and senior staff can get everyone integrated and energized for the final nearly four-month sprint. This is a time for the nominee to make sure the absolute best, most experienced veteran strategists are handling the campaign, now that virtually the whole Democratic universe is available to serve its needs. It is also a convenient place to coordinate legally with the Super PACS and labor unions and other groups; the value of having all the key representatives physically in one space, talking privately together, cannot be overstated. And the campaign also can take advantage of the Milwaukee location to recruit Wisconsin-based volunteers, to help secure a state that could decide the outcome of the election.

When the DNC settled on Milwaukee to host the convention back in March 2019, there was some grumbling and head-scratching about the choice. Milwaukee is a relatively small city, with only a modest number of hotel rooms, amenities, and entertainment spots for the revelry that accompanies delegates, special interest cadres, personnel and volunteers, and international press. Now, the strategists say, if the nominee and the party can pull off a successful convention in Milwaukee, they actually could end up with an edge in the key battleground state, a huge advantage in a race against Trump.

The following month, from August 24 to August 27, the Republicans will hold their convention in North Carolina. "Yeah," says one Democratic strategist, "North Carolina is probably out of our reach anyway."

PART IV
FALL

"LIFE STARTS ALL
OVER AGAIN WHEN IT
GETS CRISP IN THE FALL."
— F. SCOTT FITZGERALD

CHAPTER TEN
BLACK SWANS

LESSON: TRUMP WANTS
CHAOS AT THE END.

"**Y**ou, the American people, I talk to you today about the best way to avoid another catastrophe and about war, its reasons, and its consequences."

It was October 29, 2004, only four days before the contest between President George W. Bush and John Kerry would be decided. The race had been fraught and caustic, and the polls were tight. One of President Bush's most ardent critics, graying, stern, a veteran of political warfare, was making his plea, staring directly into the camera. In his view, Bush's use of military force in the Middle East after the terrorist attacks of September 11, 2001, was an immoral mistake, one that made the United States and the world less safe, and called into question Bush's character and judgment. Many Americans agreed with him.

"I say to you that security is an important pillar of human life," he continued, "and that free people do not compromise their security."

The video was initially broadcast on just one channel, but word of its existence and content spread quickly across the media and onto the presidential campaign trail.

"Although we are ushering in the fourth year after 9/11," said Osama bin Laden, "Bush is still exercising confusion and misleading you."

As October Surprises go, this one was a humdinger. Here was America's Public Enemy Number One, a globally reviled terrorist who had not been seen or heard from since February 11, 2003, appearing less than one hundred hours before Election Day to criticize and menace the commander-in-chief.

The media, collectively reeling, declared that this would probably doom Kerry's chances. Taken literally, bin Laden's words seemed intended to harm the president's bid for a second term, but the video created a reverse effect. Bush had built his reelection rationale on being the stronger national security candidate, and now the mastermind of the deadliest terrorist attack in United States history was endorsing his opponent— the ultimate backhanded compliment for the Democrat.

The press has traditionally called such events "October Surprises," but in the era of Trump, they are more aptly known as "black swans," unforeseen, sudden incidents with enormous consequences. Some Democrats fear black swans in 2020 above almost anything else; they say the Democratic nominee must be ready for them because they play to Trump's strengths. The president doesn't just thrive on chaos but seeks it out and welcomes it in.

As for bin Laden, his abrupt appearance was unexpected and entirely startling. He had gone to ground for well over a year, and there had been wild speculation about his whereabouts and the state of his health. It was even rumored that he had died. And yet here he was, alive and seemingly well, sinister and imposing, ready to disrupt the psychic balance of the country on the eve of the presidential election.

For the incumbent, the response was easy. He was resolute, determined, bipartisan, and assured. "Let me make this very clear," said Bush. "Americans will not be intimidated or influenced by an enemy of our country. I'm sure Senator Kerry agrees with this. I also want to say to the American people that we're at war with these terrorists and I am confident that we will prevail."

Leveraging the benefits of incumbency, White House officials told the press the following morning that the president, who had been campaigning in Columbus, Ohio, had conducted a videoconference with his national security advisors from his hotel room to determine if the bin Laden message suggested the possibility of imminent attacks against the United States. They also said the commander-in-chief had ordered the FBI, CIA, and other agencies to take all required steps to protect the homeland.

Kerry struggled to formulate a reply. Any chance of delivering his prepared closing argument to the voters was now impossible. All anyone was talking about now was the bin Laden video and how it would impact the election. Kerry would be asked about it every time he spoke to the media.

Over the next twenty-four hours, Kerry gave several different replies, sometimes hewing closely to Bush's initial message of bipartisan solidarity. But his first response, and then another the following day, were more political, using the video as an opening to criticize Bush's record.

"As I have said for two years now," Kerry declared in Appleton, Wisconsin, "when Osama bin Laden and Al-Qaeda were cornered in the mountains of Tora Bora, it was wrong to outsource the job to Afghan warlords who a week earlier were fighting against us, instead of using the best-trained troops in the world who wanted to avenge America for what happened in New York and Pennsylvania and in Washington. It was wrong to divert our forces from Afghanistan so we could rush to war without a plan to win the peace."

George W. Bush was not, in any way, fundamentally or unapologetically shameless like Donald Trump, but he knew an opportunity when he saw one. As a politician, a favorite trick of his was to score points by accusing his adversary, with faux indignation, of trying to score points. He called Kerry's Appleton remarks disgraceful and played up his own national security credentials, further exercising the benefits of incumbency.

Long after Bush won the election, with a narrow 50.7 percent popular vote win and 286 electoral votes, both campaigns said that his victory, in retrospect, rested in part on the release of the tape and Kerry's flawed reaction to it. The strategists use this as a prime example of how to handle, and not handle, the black swans that will inevitably glide into the final weeks of the general election campaign. The strategists caution that there may be a circumstance when true leadership is required, and the entire country will actively envision the candidate in the White House. When this arises, the Democrat should prepare a strong response, remain dignified and patriotic, avoid self-serving statements, and use subtlety when going on the attack against Trump. Above all, the challenger must remember that Trump will play dirty, no matter how grave the threat or sober the event.

The manner in which the nominee reacts to black swans, says John Sasso, will go a long way toward determining if her or his candidacy is upended in the closing days. Kerry, he says, did the exact opposite of what was required.

"Let's put it this way," Sasso explains. "Instead of saying, 'Look, the one thing we're not going to allow to happen is, and George Bush and I agree on this, and all Americans should agree, we are not going to let that despicable person interfere in our elections, which is clearly what [bin Laden is] trying to do with less than a week to go. Neither of us should in any way try to use this for an advantage. We should be united and say "you will not interfere in our elections"' and that would have been reinforcing strength and conviction as opposed to looking political on something that shouldn't be handled politically."

Furthermore, says Sasso, Kerry "should not have made it about himself, not try to take advantage. Look, you're always looking for ways to take advantage. But I think in the larger sense, the way to take advantage of a person like Trump and the contrast you want to draw with him is to be less overtly political. And cognizant of bringing the country together. That should be your first instinct, not your last."

No matter whom the Democrats nominate, the strategists are unanimous in predicting that the fall of 2020 will be filled with twists and turns; September, October, and November Surprises; and a bevy of black swans, some of which could be as serious as the one Kerry confronted.

For one thing, there is just something about Donald Trump that naturally attracts black swans into his orbit. For another, the Democrats have no doubt that Trump, who himself is so unpredictable, will use Twitter and the powers of the presidency to create some synthetic black swans, to the same effect as those that occur organically.

Warns Donna Brazile, "Trump is going to control the message. Trump is going to be Donald Trump."

"2020 is going to be the year of the black swan," says another strategist. "Look what happened in 2016. *Access Hollywood*, WikiLeaks, Putin, Comey, Anthony Weiner. Even Trump was thrown for a loop half the time, although he instinctively knew when to be quiet. And this time, he is going to know how to take better advantage and make it all as messy as possible, because then he is in his element."

"The way you lose to Trump," says Tad Devine, "is Trump turns this into what in Providence we would call a 'frittata.' It's like scrambled eggs. You're going to throw it all into the pot and kind of mix it all up. You don't want to do that. The confusion is my biggest concern. Trump wants confusion. He's sowing confusion. He's always going to be there with the next thing, constantly. We want to have order. He wants noise. He's looking to create noise. You've got to be extremely disciplined in terms of message delivery."

Larry Grisolano is sympathetic to the travails the Democrat will be facing, especially during such a heated, stressful period. "The first thing is, it's hard," he acknowledges. "You can't manage the information environment the way you are used to, and you have got to be prepared to live with that, rather than be more in the mind-set of, 'okay, how are we going to control this?'"

In the closing days, the closing hours, if Trump thinks he is losing, he will not merely accept his fate. He will do everything he can to generate one or more distractions so immense that the entire environment is transformed for those still casting their ballots. Trump did not cause Comey to intercede twice in the two weeks before Election Day, but he knows he probably owes his victory to the former FBI director. That experience suggests to the strategists that Trump will exploit his position to launch seismic events that could once again put him over the top in the campaign's final days. And Trump's relative rhetorical restraint in the aftermath of Comey's two revelations on Clinton's email probe also indicates that he can enforce a particular self-discipline and step to the sidelines when the blistering glare of the spotlight is on his opponent.

Hillary Clinton was essentially powerless to counteract Comey's machinations, and Democrats are concerned that history will repeat itself in 2020. The strategists can conjure any number of alarming scenarios. Some express worry that Trump's allies will do his bidding, pointing as an example to the 2018 Georgia gubernatorial election, in which the Republicans' victorious candidate was still serving as secretary of state and oversaw the election process during the campaign. Democrat Stacey Abrams charged that several thousand people were improperly deemed ineligible to vote, while more than 50,000 people had their voter registrations delayed without sufficient notice from

the government. Both actions, Democrats allege, had a dispro-
portionate impact on African American voters.

LaBolt says, "Number one, I think Republicans are going to
organize what they did in Georgia against Stacey Abrams in
every battleground state where they are in power. I don't think
an election protection effort, where we just go stand at the
polls on Election Day, is sufficient."

LaBolt and others fear that Trump and his supporters will
use these election-eve battles to sow confusion and discord,
potentially suppressing some Democratic votes and giving the
incumbent a black swan justification to reject the results at the
ballot box if they are not in his favor. The Democrats will have
to install teams of lawyers and communication specialists to
sort fact from fiction and to keep Trump from capitalizing on
any chaos his own side initiates.

"I strongly believe the Trump campaign will engage in an
'ends justify the means' campaign," says Jennifer Granholm.
"It's why they are still inviting foreign influence in the elections—it's obvious that winning is far more important than an
election free from Russian hackers. It's why they will be deploying all manner of fake news stories, misdirection, lies, and
voter suppression—at the ballot box or via social media—to
persuade Democrats to stay home, vote for a third party, or
skip the top of the ballot like they did in Michigan in 2016."

The strategists do not doubt that Trump will call upon all
the functions of his office to render an embellished image of
his presidency. "On a very basic level, he will have the advantages of incumbency," says Brian Fallon. "He will be able to
look the part as he runs the campaign. He will be able to even
more than in 2016 exercise control over the news of the day
because he will have the power of the office. So more than just
making provocative statements to try to define the debate,
he'll be able to carry out executive actions, orders to agencies
to do things. He can announce there's going to be some big

immigration roundup and people won't know if it is true or not, but they'll have to treat it as such because he is the president saying that something is going to happen. He can likewise do things on the international stage that would force people to react. So it will be more than just bluster that will be provocative, which got him a long way in 2016. Now he will be able to back up provocative talk with provocative actions. It will have even more of an effect in terms of riling up his supporters, but also just trying to define the scope of the conversation."

Other strategists think Trump might toss tradition and decorum out the window and juice the economy right after Labor Day, with a slick trick such as firing the chair of the Federal Reserve Board or striking a Hail Mary trade pact with China. Trump knows full well that he can pull some levers to prod the stock market and give him both a talking point and a strong close.

Also on the list of strategist concerns: claims of voter suppression against Trump supporters and allegations of widespread voter fraud by non-white voters. Or a classic "wag the dog" military action that would completely dominate news coverage, sweep aside the Democrat's message, and highlight the imbalance in status between the two candidates.

"He can also carry out nefarious actions," says Fallon. "I think it's a legitimate concern that he would instruct or urge the Justice Department to carry out at least preliminary investigations into his opponent or people connected to his opponent in order to sort of create a cloud over them. Basically replicate the circumstances that worked to his advantage in 2016 with the email investigation into Hillary." The administration could leak word of the existence of these probes, or escalate them shortly before Election Day.

"Take the craziest scenarios we've planned for in the past," says LaBolt, "and I think we need to multiply by ten with this election."

The strategists believe that some of Trump's gambits will be meant to serve two purposes simultaneously. They will be intended to help his chances of winning by the initial count of votes. But they also could be used to deliberately undermine the legitimacy of the results in the battleground states and allow him to claim that the system was rigged against him by the establishment, the deep state, the bureaucracy, the Democrats, and the media, and refuse to yield the White House to the actual winner.

Says LaBolt, "I think every Republican state attorney general in a battleground state is going to be Katherine Harris this time around," referencing the Florida election official who Democrats viewed as giving George W. Bush an improper assist during the 2000 recount.

Fallon also worries that, as with bin Laden in 2004, and Russia in 2016, some of the black swans could swoop in from overseas. "I don't think we can discount the possibility, especially now that Trump is the incumbent president, that foreign governments may see upsides to helping him and targeting his opponent for the purposes of currying favor with him," he says.

Of course, because of the spontaneous nature of the black swan, there is no reliable way to fully prepare. But the strategists say it will be possible to anticipate and preempt some of the ill effects. Trump likely will try to manufacture various sorts of distractions, so the candidate and credible surrogates should speak in advance about such possibilities, especially those involving the powers of the federal government. The candidate and surrogates should predict publicly that Trump might refuse to leave office if declared the loser, and encourage the media to pin down Trump on the issue peremptorily.

Granholm believes the best remedy is to call out the Republicans early and often. "Democrats, now and through the election, must inoculate voters from these strategies," she says. "We should be warning people about the misinformation campaigns now and through the election. The failure of Republicans in the Senate to pass voter protection bills is an opportunity at every turn to remind people that everyone will be a target of false stories and advertisements. We must tell folks to keep their eye on trusted sources only. Then when it happens, we need to hold up the examples and say, 'This is what I'm talking about. Do not fall for it.' Hopefully by shining a light on the strategy we can at least blunt the biggest of the diversions and fake narratives. But," she adds, "Trump is the master of misdirection, lies, and false story promulgation. I only hope our megaphone can match him."

Should the black swan originate from the candidate's own past, the strategists have suggestions too. "Don't get angry about the source of the story or what people are saying about you," advises one. "Those are just distractions. Keep the explanations clear and simple. When Trump goes after you on Twitter, ignore him. Everyone will expect him to gloat. Let the voters know you are the same person they have gotten to know during the campaign, and they can trust you."

Whether the black swan has personal or global ramifications, the candidate and staff should be psychologically braced for outrageous, maddening drama. Keep in mind Amanda Renteria's admonishment to be ready to do battle with Trump with unprecedented intensity. Also, they say, keep a sense of humor and perspective. This will be a momentous time, so the candidate should do what is possible to protect the country and have faith in his or her own moral core.

Says Kathleen Sebelius, "It's the kind of thing that, if they're going to be commander-in-chief, they have to get ready for, because something totally unknown is going to come over the transom. Something that they didn't plan for, that they didn't scope out, that they don't know about, whether it's a huge natural disaster, an outbreak of a disease, some kind of foreign turmoil that suddenly throws the agenda off. And at that point, you have to react quickly. You have to trust your own judgment and move out with some degree of forcefulness and then go right back on message. They always say a disaster can make or break a governor or a president, because it's how you react in the moment where you don't get scripted, where you don't have a great plan. I think the same is true with a candidate. They should expect the worst at every point along the way. They have to have a voice. You can't poll test everything that happens. You can't wait and wring your hands. You have got to forcefully have a reaction, gut check your reaction with a couple of people, move out, do it, and then get as many of your supporters and followers to do it as possible. And then keep on message, and keep on the campaign plan."

These moments will test the courage, instincts, and fortitude of whomever the Democrats nominate. "Keep your chin up," advises one strategist. "If you get past these hurdles, you'll be better prepared for the challenges of the job." And be especially vigilant as the presidential debates approach; the strategists expect black swans to trumpet loudest when the stakes are highest. Assuming there *are* presidential debates. Some of the strategists predict that Trump will become the first president since Nixon to refuse to debate his opponent.

How to execute at the end, to make the right choices, with black swans swooping here and there, will be the stuff of history.

CHAPTER ELEVEN

THE DEBATES

LESSON: DON'T PLAY IT SAFE.

I f you are a Democrat or a member of the establishment media, chances are you thought Donald Trump's performances
in his three debates opposite Hillary Clinton was somewhere
between disastrous and disqualifying.

In addition to often looking angry and ill-prepared, Trump
generated the dominant negative story line from each debate.
In the first, he spluttered when Clinton brought up his sexist
and misogynistic comments about Alicia Machado, who had
competed in Trump's Miss USA pageant. In the second, he
was forced to address the *Access Hollywood* video, which captured him bragging about sexually assaulting women. In the
third, he refused to promise to accept the election results if
Clinton was declared the victor. "I will keep you in suspense,"
he said.

For those from the portion of planet Earth evaluating
Trump's behavior based on the normal standards of human
conduct and professional political criteria, Hillary Clinton
was the clear winner of all three events. And yet public polling,
the campaigns' own analyses, and, of course, the final outcome

suggest that the debates did not work decisively in Clinton's favor. In the context of 2020, many strategists allow that Trump was surprisingly strong at speaking on a gut level to voters, while Clinton acted as if she were trying to win a Model UN competition.

Says one Democratic communications operative, "I think the debates were misjudged a bit in real time in 2016. It was clear that Hillary was winning on policy points, but that didn't win the debates for her. So I think the assumption that white papers or policy points will win the debates is a mistake."

The lesson here, say Democratic strategists, is for the nominee to go for the knockout. Elites may have been impressed by Clinton's polish and professionalism in 2016, but in 2020 it will be smarter not to play it safe. The candidate must avoid getting bogged down in rehearsed pronouncements and stale self-promotion. Instead, he or she must embrace the term *debate*.

This does not mean the 2020 candidate should go in raw and ready to improvise. On the contrary, the debates should be approached as if applying for the All Souls fellowship at Oxford. The candidate should be fully prepared to take questions involving policy minutiae, world facts, twisty hypotheticals, past statements, gotchas, and up-to-the-minute current events, plus pop culture, personal taste, and the cost of grocery items. Good preparation will give the nominee confidence and a safety net, even if none of the expected topics is covered, and even if—especially if—the debate goes off the rails.

Trump famously did little prep for either his Republican or general election debates four years ago, and advisors concede he is unlikely to alter his routine this time around. Karen Dunn, who oversaw the preparations for Clinton and Barack Obama for their presidential debates, is confident the Democrat can gain an edge by practicing meticulously. "Prepare, prepare, prepare," she says. "He will not, unless you count eating burgers at a golf course." It is a safe bet that whomever the Democrats nominate will spend significantly more time training for the debates than will Trump.

As noted, several of the strategists envision a debate black swan, with Trump refusing to participate. They can see him making mincemeat out of the Commission on Presidential Debates, the bipartisan organizing committee that has produced the presidential debates since 1988 and decides on the dates, moderators, formats, and venues. In his typical autocratic mode, Trump might demand changes in the logistical or stylistic guidelines put forth by the Commission, inserting so many stipulations and restrictions that the debates become degraded, or inventing a pretext that leads to the black swan scenario. As Tad Devine remarks, "I have a feeling Trump may just say, 'Forget it. The debates are fixed. I don't want to do the debates.'"

Several of the strategists predicted the president could use the Commission (an establishment entity easy for Trump to demonize) to play his typical cat-and-mouse game about whether he will indeed appear, stringing along the organizers, the moderators, the media, and the competition, and kicking up dust all around. One person working for a 2020 presidential candidate notes that Trump has a made-to-order talking point on which to hang any public reluctance to submit to the Commission. Four years ago, at his first general election debate, Trump's microphone malfunctioned, making it nearly impossible for him to modulate his voice for both the live audience and those watching on TV. Trump complained about the technical problem immediately following the event and for days afterward. Hillary Clinton, meanwhile, mocked him for apparently needing to excuse away his bumpy performance.

The Commission, after initially refusing to engage on the matter, eventually put out a vague and low-key statement implicitly acknowledging that Trump had cause for grievance.

"Regarding the first debate, there were issues regarding Donald Trump's audio that affected the sound level in the debate hall," the Commission said, without elaboration.

Even though Trump sailed through the Republican debates, smirking and jousting, tossing out insults all around, he was less self-assured before the general election debates against Clinton. And despite his unconventional, arguable debate wins, Trump might be delighted to never set foot on a debate stage again. To avoid such an ordeal, and to deny his opponent a chance to shine or best him, he could easily decide he would rather take the heat for ducking the debates (using the Commission as a scapegoat) than risk humiliating himself or elevating his opponent.

If Trump initially agrees to debate, he will approach the contest aware that his Democratic rival craves the chance to stand on the stage beside him. In a general election, the debates are the only moments in which a challenger to an incumbent is on equal ground with the commander-in-chief. It is a basic Trumpian principle, says one strategist, that when Trump controls something his rival wants, he is tempted to withhold it. For all these reasons, oddsmakers in Las Vegas should hold off on taking wagers until the candidates actually step out onto the stage.

"If he plays those games," says one strategist, "we shouldn't let him get away with it. Drive home to the American people that he's the one calling the thing off. Make him pay a price." Still, the strategist admits that Trump would likely stir up a noisy, convenient distraction and brush aside the criticism anyway. But Devine believes the point should be pressed hard. "If Trump starts to back out of the debates," he says, "the Democratic nominee should go immediately before television cameras and in a strong voice and manner call him out for being weak and afraid."

Trump also might use similar tactics to limit his participation to just one or two debates, rather than the three that have become the norm over the last several decades. John Sasso feels the Democrat should then make it clear that Trump is afraid of exposing his own inadequacies and limitations. "I think you have to use it to undermine his strength and conviction," says Sasso. "If he was what he claims to be, he wouldn't be afraid to get up on this stage. It's the same when he says he'll do this thing, or he'll testify under oath [to Robert Mueller]. And then, of course, he always walks away from it because he's afraid. Because he is really not a strong person."

A few strategists, however, entirely reject the idea that Trump will try to dodge debates. "That's such a chicken move," says Jennifer Granholm. "It would be so obvious that he's afraid of whoever the nominee is and of his record that he can't even stand on the same stage. I just can't see him doing that. I can't imagine him tolerating being called a coward when he is all bluster."

So, let us assume for the moment that Granholm is correct, and Trump will participate in three debates. The strategists robustly advise the Democratic nominee to take some lessons from Hillary Clinton's 2016 campaign—on what not to do.

The Clinton team chose to hold debate prep at the Doral Arrowwood, a conference center in Rye Brook, New York, just a few miles from Clinton's Westchester County home. Politicos universally condemned this decision. Rather than allow the campaign to base its debate camp in a battleground state, Clinton preferred to work close to her home in Chappaqua. In 2000, Al Gore did some of his preparatory work in all-important Florida, while in 2012, Barack Obama held mock sessions with his staff in Virginia. In both cases, the venues were chosen so the candidates could fit in public campaign events between practice times to garner press coverage in the media market and the state.

Countless decisions contributed to Clinton's defeat, but among the most exasperating to the strategists was the failure to locate her debate prep operation in, say, Wisconsin or Pennsylvania, a simple switch that, no exaggeration, could have made her president.

So that is an easy one. If the nominee has to spend three or four days straight in the same place just weeks before Election Day, by all means pick a battleground state. Once that is done, says Bob Shrum, who has participated in prep for any number of presidential hopefuls, the candidate should begin the process by thinking about how to shape the central themes of the debate. Only then should briefing books be distributed and mock debates commence.

Shrum also stresses the need to strictly limit the number of people giving the candidate feedback during and after sessions, in order to greatly reduce the chance of mixed messages, frustration, confusion, or overload. The candidate should be well prepared but not overwhelmed. When under the bright lights, facing the moderators' queries, the answers should come cleanly.

Debate prep rooms are intensely fraught places. The candidate is a nervous wreck, the staff overworked and frantic, and, just beyond the doors, the media is relentless, with growing anticipation and the pile-on of never-ending polls and speculation. The mock sessions involve a surrogate standing in for the opponent, tapped for resemblance and style, dressed with precision, and affecting an accent or familiar habitual ticks. These performances are often award-worthy. In 2012, patrician Massachusetts politician John Kerry played patrician Massachusetts politician Mitt Romney. In 2016, Clinton's right-hand aide, Philippe Reines, went so far as to wear lifts in his shoes, velcro pads on his knees, and a brace on his back to replicate Trump's imposing height and lumbering posture, on top of months of intensive rehearsal.

It is astonishing how often the candidates get lost in the role play, becoming not just flustered but downright angry, lashing out as if being attacked by an actual foe, and forgetting entirely that the room is filled with sympathetic allies there to help. "It's a vulnerable experience," says one strategist who has been present at several preps. "Here is a candidate seeking the presidency, and then all their weaknesses, their personal flaws, their embarrassing blind spots of basic knowledge, all exposed. They don't like being knocked around and challenged. And that's exactly the reason these sessions are so important."

Hillary Clinton was certainly well prepared. But her decision to play it safe in the debates, say the strategists, was evidence of her campaign's certitude that she was on a glide path to victory and therefore had no reason to take risks. In 2020, the strategists unanimously agree, a dignified but aggressive approach is the way to go, in large part because Trump is a bully. He thrives when he can stage-manage and dominate but wilts when put on the defensive. In a debate, most of the factors are beyond his control, which leaves him off-balance and potentially a little timid. This offers an opportunity for his opponent to apply a unique pressure that no member of Congress, journalist, or foreign leader is able to do. One-on-one, under the microscope, millions watching breathlessly, Trump will be forced to think on his feet without fundamentally changing the rules to suit his impulses. Expect him to rely on intimidation, bluster, interruptions, unpredictability, and mulish falsehoods.

As Shrum puts it, Trump "is perfectly capable of saying almost anything, and acting up, and looming over you, and coming over to your podium, and all that kind of stuff." One of Hillary Clinton's advisors, Adrienne Elrod, offers a key point: "Because the guy has no fear, you can't be nervous around him. You can't be worried about how he's going to react to certain things that you say, certain things that you do." Karen Dunn warns, "To make up for a lack of debate skills he may pull stunts or say outlandish things." She cites the second presidential debate, when Trump invited women who had accused Bill Clinton of sexual misconduct and assault to attend the event and seated them prominently in the audience.

These gambits only work, says Dunn, if the Democrat gets shaken. Dunn has studied Trump's past debates as closely as anyone in the party and she remains fundamentally unimpressed. "Donald Trump," she says flatly, "is not a good debater," in part because "he is entirely predictable." Therefore, she beseeches the Democrat not to get psyched out by the Trump mystique. "If you put in the time to prep, you will walk onto the stage with a man whose every move you have predicted, who is not, by raw talent, a particularly good debater." She strongly recommends that the nominee recruit Reines to reprise his role as Trump in debate prep. Reines got uniformly high marks from his colleagues for being "eerily good" at channeling Trump, including all the billionaire's predictable mannerisms, intrusions, and replies.

Even Chris Christie, Trump's competitor for the 2016 nomination who helped his longtime friend prepare for the general election debates, sees a fundamental flaw in the incumbent's game. The former New Jersey governor told Stephen Colbert in 2019 that Trump's "biggest weakness" is that he swings "at every pitch. He can't let anything go by. He swings at the ball in the dirt, he swings at the ball over his head. Last time, he was kind of Teflon on that; no matter what he said, it didn't matter." This time, Christie suggests, things will be different. Trump will finally be held to a more normal standard.

It is going to be up to the Democrat to take advantage when Trump is flailing. The consensus view is that Trump is most vulnerable to a debater who can make him seem angry, mentally unfit, or faithless to his campaign promises. "I think that hitting a tone where you are pushing back and you are taking on his behavior using ridicule without going too snarky" is the way to go, says one strategist. Reveal who Trump truly is, she adds, and take an "I am rubber, you are glue, whatever you say is going to bounce off me and stick to you" approach.

Kamala Harris advisor Jim Margolis identifies one of Trump's great frailties.

"First and foremost," he says, "there are some people who are just great communicators. They have a combination of strength and warmth. Trump has zero warmth. Zero empathy. And for the voters you need to move to win, that's a problem. He has strength, but if you can find a candidate who can connect with people on a personal level while at the same time demonstrating they have the muscle to take on this big guy who thrives on baiting opponents with dismissive, rude, and disrespectful exchanges—that's a pretty good combination."

Many veteran operatives think Trump is far more fragile than he appears, an old-school bully, a coddled older man recently subjected to the unique, unavoidable pressures of the Oval Office. Says Alper, "You might really be able to get him undone. I've wondered about his health, his mental health, and constitution [being laid bare at] the highest inflection point in any campaign when you have the two candidates standing next to each other."

While Clinton failed to connect with a knockout punch, Alper says, Trump "hadn't been president for a number of years. He wasn't up all night, at the end of his rope. There's more evidence that has come out. It is a calculated risk, but I think this time around, with a more confident and aggressive debater," Trump could be embarrassed in a way that alters the outcome. With some clever and calculated maneuvers, and some well-played mind games, the Democrat could shove him over the edge.

"Everything about him is, 'He's the tough guy, he's in charge,' right?" Alper posits. "We keep trying to beat him with words. It is possible that we can show this man is not temperamentally fit. I think that that could be a big moment." But, she says, it will take considerable effort in prep to plan for that occasion. "And what are the odds that you can do that?" she wonders.

In the case of Trump, say the strategists, the odds are not bad, given his egomania, entitlement, and self-indulgence. As Devine says, "Here's a guy getting his ass kissed his whole life." Donna Brazile asserts, "He wants to be the toughest guy in the room. He wants to be the meanest guy in the room. He wants to be the most combative. He wants to be the bully." Many of the experts warm to the theme of discombobulating the incumbent and cutting him down to size.

"Presidents get used to being president," Ben LaBolt says. "There's an opportunity to rattle Trump and knock him off his game and show his anger. He has certainly been angry at the media as president, but being angry over being questioned is not a good look for a president. And I think that's an area of vulnerability for Trump."

Says Mike McCurry, "How do you get him to go to his worst points, his narcissistic focus on himself and then say, 'Donald, it's not about you, it's about America'?"

Shrum agrees that the way to break Trump is to create a big, *ooh-ahh* moment, a point the former TV host would understand viscerally. "You can't imitate him," Shrum says, "but you can call him to account. You can probably anticipate the kinds of things he is going to do in a debate, and you can get ready for them. And this is the place where a put-down line, if it resonates with voters, can be very powerful."

A few of the strategists singled out the lone Carter-Reagan debate in 1980, in which Reagan reeled off two sound bites ("There you go again" and "Are you better off than you were four years ago?") that still echo through history today. One or two cutting lines such as those, particularly if they occur in the first (or only) debate, could whittle Trump down to size in a way that transforms the race.

James Carville suggests the Democratic nominee go straight in for the kill with the very first exchange between the candidates, no matter what the question. "I would say this: 'I want to be very clear. If I'm elected president, I'm going to appoint an independent, thoughtful, and qualified attorney general. And I'm going to ask that attorney general to report to me in thirty days. And if he or she thinks this president committed crimes, then we are going to pursue it. If not, if he or she tells me that it's okay, then we won't. But, sir, we are going to take a fresh look at all this, particularly the obstruction side.' That's what I'd say. And watch him go fucking crazy. First answer in the first debate."

It is possible, say the strategists, that Trump's appeal to his base can be undermined by exposing him as a fraud. Says Pete Giangreco, "He's tough on everything, right? That's his brand. 'I'm the tough guy. I'm the one, I'm the one. I'm indispensable. No one else is going to take on China. I'm the one that's going to take on Mexico. I'm the one that's going to build the wall. I'm indispensable. And it is my toughness that you need.' And what we are saying is, that's not toughness—that's recklessness and he is endangering the economic security of farmers, auto workers, anybody in the Detroit suburbs that has anything to do with the automotive industry, this guy is a threat to you."

Once Trump's perceived fortitude is recast as foolhardiness, his whole persona can be redefined by the Democrat, who will thereby have seized control of Trump's public image, the ultimate debate trophy. Especially if the Democrat can keep a cool head. Larry Grisolano says, "I think that the way to disarm him is to look mature next to his childishness and not take the bait. I just think that if people feel like there might be a calmer haven out there amid the chaos, that that's going to be appealing."

"Not being fooled again is a really important thread, I think," says Granholm. "Whoever the nominee is, that is the thread they should pull. 'He did this before,' you can call it out in a meta sort of way. 'You can see what he's doing. He's trying to fool you. He's trying to distract. And we are not going to do it.' Respond with humor, maybe, in some instances. In some instances, with anger."

All the strategists make it clear that the Democrat, in the debates as in the overall campaign, should not emulate Trump's unscrupulous character. No engaging in a volley of insults or ad hominem attacks, they say. But sharp exchanges that aim to expose Trump's less attractive personality traits or policy shortcomings could decisively change the trajectory of the race, rousing base and swing voters alike. If the Democrat pulled off a true strike, the strategists are certain the media would pounce, replaying and discussing it again and again, along with Trump's reaction to it.

Remaining principled does not mean the Democrat should avoid getting personal. Charlie Baker suggests bringing up legitimate controversies involving Trump's children, about which he has shown sensitivity in the past. "You have to make Trump look small and weak and petty," Baker says, and once his hackles are raised, chances are Trump will end up playing defense.

Recalling Sasso's list of traits a successful presidential candidate must convey is useful at this juncture. A Democrat who evinces strength, conviction, and empathy can land a vicious blow without seeming vicious. "If you sink to his level, then he'll win because he's the best at that level," Sasso says. "You have to have a certain integrity and strength. Stand up to him firmly to point out when he is embellishing things and lying about things. Then pivot to your own pitch right away. You cannot let him in any way dominate the dialogue or dominate you or dismiss you. You have got to show a strong personality that will take him on, but take him on in a dignified, honest way."

There is a difference between challenging Trump, agrees Bill Carrick, and mud wrestling with him. Accusing him, in a high-minded manner and tone, of misleading the American people is what is required to go for the kill. Do not talk about defending America's institutions. Talk about protecting America's families, Carrick says.

Carville offers this: "What I would say is, 'You know this man. He's been the president of this country for almost four years. I don't want to talk about him. The first thing I want to do as president of the United States is to get my hands on that thermostat, and I'm going to turn it down. We are just going to ratchet our language and our actions down. And he's free to do any antics he wants; he's free to talk to his base. I wanna talk to the country.' I just wouldn't fuck with him. I wouldn't fuck with him at all."

Agrees David Axelrod, "In keeping with my basic premise," that Trump is a toxic agent of chaos who is sapping the nation, "my debate strategy would be jujitsu. Do not reflect Trump's negative energy. Use it against him."

All the communication imperatives from earlier in the campaign, especially at the convention, apply to the debates as well. Do not snub or condescend to Trump supporters. Focus on the core message and issues where there is a marked advantage over Trump. Project anger about the status quo but optimism about the future.

Karen Dunn argues that a key to winning the TV or streaming audience is to appear to be having fun on the debate stage, no matter how tense things grow. Trump may make a few cracks to get the live audience laughing, but he likely can be counted on to glower and glare at both the moderators and his opponent. Answer his grim countenance with above-the-fray smiles and signals of carefree relaxation, suggests Dunn.

Shrum says the candidate needs to remember that the cutaway camera and the two-shot will be documenting every facial expression even when it is Trump's turn to talk. That means no scowling or over-modulated reactions. If Trump makes an outrageous statement, lobs a personal insult, or does anything that might induce a bad visual response, the Democrat should blankly look at a pad or the microphone and pretend to take some notes. "Never betray that he can get to you," says a strategist. "That will give him power. Always be unflappable. Look placid, don't smirk, never roll your eyes. Don't pretend to be indifferent, just be bland. If he goes after you personally, who cares? This is Donald Trump. Who cares what he thinks of you?"

And there should be no laurel-resting once the debate is over. On several occasions in 2016, immediately after a debate ended, Trump strode into the spin room for rope-line chats with reporters and some formal interviews. He was upbeat and engaged, and always claimed victory. Several strategists recommend that the Democrat likewise enter the spin room for a victory lap to establish that she or he can go head to head with Trump and emerge tenacious.

A few of the strategists have other suggestions about how to make best use of the spin room both before and after the debate, including replacing the typical surrogate politicians and breathless, hyperbolic staffers with another wave of the "real people" who were deployed at the convention. "I would avoid sending a bunch of the so-called spin doctors and pundits into cable studios and the spin room," says LaBolt. "I would think about some [former] Trump voters who moved away from Trump because they're disappointed that he didn't live up to his promises. People in states affected by his policies who got hammered by the tariffs or who are paying higher taxes while corporations are paying [less]." The citizen spinners should be compelling and specific, have clear explanations about why they regret their 2016 vote for Trump, and be able to comment, post-debate, on how the president's arguments, performance, and promises fell short yet again.

"If there are people who voted for Trump and who have been adversely affected," says Granholm, "and who are willing to bear witness now, in the same way that Trump brought all those former Bill Clinton women to the debate, I think a Democrat can bring people like that—former Trump people from the industrial Midwest or from farm and rural areas who are willing to stand up and say, 'I was conned. This man is a fraud. I am not voting for him. He's bad for us.' So using those testimonials, I think, is really important."

The campaign's staff should be prepared to manage the social media front, before, during, and after the debates, primarily on Twitter, to influence the views and analysis of political reporters. These one-on-one candidate showdowns are subjective things, with many variables shifting simultaneously; the way an exchange plays inside the hall versus outside, the personal biases each journalist carries, the verbal intonations and facial flickers onstage that might be missed while typing a note or gulping a coffee or, well, scrolling through Twitter.

Hundreds of texts and emails fly between reporters—*What do you think?*—since the stakes are so high for the candidates and for the press, and few are willing to risk getting it wrong. Many reporters want some reassurance that history will validate their interpretation, and that they will not be mocked on the Internet. If a staffer can whisper in an ear, plant a seed in a brain, make a convincing case, then the whole narrative can be manipulated in the Democrat's favor.

The campaign staff should also use all social media platforms to reach voters in targeted areas and demographics on a massive scale. And the content should be as creative and customized as possible, an enormous task to be sure, but one that can reap untold Election Day rewards. "Many voters will watch these debates," says one strategist, "but many more won't and they will want to know what happened. They'll see news reports, and video replays of the big moments. But this is a time when they will be open to hearing what the campaigns think. If you can reach them fast, that will influence them going forward. Whether you have gaffes you want to laugh off, or facts you want to clarify, or if Trump makes a mistake, and you want to give that another punch."

But, the strategist adds, "don't be too over-the-top about it. If you just brag or get preachy, voters will ignore it as annoying spin. Do a short, careful recap that hits the points each group cares about the most. I would advise taking almost a neutral tone, as long as the whole message elevates the Democrat." The message should be one of competence and might, to rally base voters, shape the media story line, and convince everyone the Democrat surpassed Trump as a leader.

The strategists all agree that the most important debate guideline is basic Trump 101: Debate, then, win or lose, declare victory.

"Whatever happens, no matter what happens, you won," says one advisor. "Unless you get out on the stage, freeze up, and don't utter a word. And maybe even then. You won."

CHAPTER TWELVE
270 WINS

LESSON: PLAY OFFENSE,
BUT PLAY IT WISELY.

Congratulations to the Democratic 2020 presidential nominee, who has made it past the primaries without losing integrity, soul, or heart; veepstakes, without picking a lemon; the convention, without sparking a party implosion; the start of the general election, without getting trumped by wild cards or being pecked to shreds by a black swan; and the debates, without falling off the stage. The early and absentee voting has been progressing smoothly, and the country is getting ready to line up at the polls.

Further kudos for empathizing with Trump's supporters; differentiating between the president's kooky antics and his virtuoso political skills; safeguarding that all-important public image; raising bounteous cash; finding a comfortable rhythm; and elevating the game.

And all this while Team Trump leveraged a nearly four-year head start to construct a well-financed political death star designed specifically to prevent any of these achievements.

But winning the presidency is both a right-brain and a left-brain proposition. Finessing frenemies; acing debates;

dodging insults and exposés; courting party chieftains, citizens, and citizens, and press; confronting Donald Trump—all meaningless without pulling in the cold, hard numbers.

This is what Paul Tully, the disheveled, brilliant, beloved Democratic data guru, knew all those years ago when he helped a young Bill Clinton map out a believable path to the White House.

If the Democrat has done the job correctly, then the campaign will be positioned to focus on the only challenge that remains: winning 270 electoral votes. Already, the strategists are gaming out the vote count. One group says it is possible for the Democrat to mobilize progressives; scoop up the alienated farmers and white working-class voters who are affronted by the president's for-the-rich economic policies; and bring in suburban women who have been displeased by Trump's nonstop chaos and blatant appeals to race and racism.

This group envisions winning the states Hillary Clinton won in 2016 (California, Colorado, Connecticut, Delaware, Hawaii, Illinois, Maine, Maryland, Massachusetts, Minnesota, Nevada, New Hampshire, New Jersey, New Mexico, New York, Oregon, Rhode Island, Vermont, Virginia, Washington, plus D.C.), adding Michigan, Pennsylvania, and Wisconsin, and also taking Florida, North Carolina, Georgia, Arizona, Texas, and all of Maine (which splits its electoral votes by congressional district). That would be 388 electoral votes for the Democrat to just 150 for Trump—a landslide. And that does not even include capturing Ohio and Iowa, states that Obama won twice.

Bearish Democratic strategists, however, worry that Trump can offset any 2016 voters he loses by increasing rural and white working-class turnout in his favor and adding incremental support from African Americans, Hispanics, and Asian Americans. These pessimistic strategists believe they can probably hold all the Clinton states, but fear they are unlikely to take Florida, North Carolina, Arizona, Texas, the Maine congressional district Trump won in 2016, Ohio, or Iowa, and in trying would squander valuable resources better applied to the more winnable battlegrounds of Pennsylvania, Michigan, and Wisconsin. The bullish Democrats are confident this last trio, the Big 3, are, separately and together, easily within range, with the right amount of effort.

"I think it comes down to eight states," longtime union and political strategist Steve Rosenthal says. "Deny Trump Colorado, New Mexico, New Hampshire, and Virginia, which is one grouping in my mind, and then Michigan, Wisconsin, Pennsylvania, and Minnesota, and he can't win. There's no path to 270 electoral votes without at least one of those states."

This is a valid argument, although it leaves the Democrats no margin of error. The loss of any of the electoral votes of Michigan, Pennsylvania, or Wisconsin would flip a 278-260 Democratic win to Trump and return him to the White House. Additionally, this scenario necessitates that potential Republican efforts to take Minnesota, New Hampshire, Nevada, New Mexico, and perhaps, Oregon, Virginia, or Colorado are all unsuccessful. While Trump won Pennsylvania, Michigan, and Wisconsin by the narrowest of margins in 2016, many strategists believe he is fully capable of winning all three of them again.

In 2016, Clinton fought to win Pennsylvania, spending copious resources and holding many events in the state, although her campaign mostly took Michigan and Wisconsin for granted. Now, the strategists fret that just because the Democrats know they will have to put in the work this time does not mean victory is automatic.

Wisconsin is of particular concern. Although Obama won it easily both times, it has produced competitive, one-percent-margin contests in many statewide races. And in recent elections, when both political parties and their allies targeted it vociferously, Republicans have often come out on top. Of all the must-win battleground states, says Charlie Baker, "The trickiest one is Wisconsin."

Rosenthal takes the point a step further. "Honestly, I think the whole thing comes down to Wisconsin, if you want to know the truth," he says. "It is the center of the storm."

• • •

So Election Day, Priority Number One?

The Big 3: Wisconsin, Pennsylvania, and Michigan.

Both the Republican and Democratic sides will be competing fiercely, and using all available resources, to win these states. The Democratic candidates should be playing the long game from primary season onward; every house party, rally, radio call-in, and hearty handshake should have November 3 in mind.

After that, the choices for the Democratic camp get more complicated. There must be a solid defensive strategy in the states that Clinton won in 2016 and Trump is targeting in 2020. And there must be an aggressive offensive strategy to get 270 votes, should one or more of the Big 3 go to the president. "There's some vulnerability in Colorado, New Hampshire, and Minnesota, which are Blue battleground states," says a strategist. "The Democrats need to lock those down as early as possible," and allocate necessary collateral, in case Trump sees an opportunity. "It's absolutely vital," the strategist maintains.

If the challenger can open up big enough leads, the Republicans will not waste money competing in those states, and the Democrats will therefore not have to spend money shoring them up, or have to expend the most valuable commodity— candidate campaign visits—in the final weeks before Election Day. Otherwise, the campaign will be throwing away time and money. It's the electoral version of the routine maintenance a homeowner does to avoid having to replace an entire roof.

One experienced strategist warns that regardless of which battlegrounds are actually in danger, the Republicans will "try to use money to either force Democrats to move into states that they think are safer at this point, or at least make them really nervous about not doing it. And playing into the psychosis that a lot of Democrats have about what they think was or was not done in 2016, leaving some states on the map, not contesting other states, all of those things."

Tad Devine believes a dynamic offensive game is crucial. "I would try to figure out if there are some opportunities to go into some states that Trump won last time by more than just a few votes," he says. "I think it would absolutely freak the guy out. If he thinks he is going to be losing states that he won last time, there is a very good chance that he will start pouring inordinate amounts of resources into some places that they don't need to. I think that's one thing that is worth trying to figure out. Depending on who the nominee is, it could be Arizona, or Georgia, or Texas. I think you have to force them to spend resources or they are going to be setting the playing field. Once he gets you in the passive position, you lose."

Sebelius, an early supporter of Obama in his first run for the White House as a Red state governor from Kansas, appreciates how Obama's team made smart, analytical decisions when prospecting for new targets. "I watched the 2008 campaign do incredibly well, starting with a very wide swath [of possible additional battlegrounds] and have clear metrics about what states needed to do in terms of voter registration, organization, money raising, and whatever else, in order to keep that wide swath of states on the map," she says.

Most of the strategists, however, advise discretion about expanding the competitive map into states that look promising but are fool's gold. Georgia, Arizona, and Texas get talked about all the time because the demographic changes there have produced a more diverse electorate and because much of the media is fascinated by the prospect of a Democratic presidential candidate fundamentally reshaping the balance of power by winning one of those previously solid-Red Sunbelt mega-states.

But every dollar or day spent in those states, or even in Florida or Ohio, is a dollar and a day away from the Big 3 and the Hillary states that are more likely to form the winning combination. Says Ben LaBolt, "I don't think we should go on any Don Quixote quests into Texas, unless there are six months of polling that says we're up by five percent."

"Personally, I am not big into expanding," says Charlie Baker. "I don't think you need to radically expand the playing field. I think you can tie Trump down and push" on the core states.

Mellman says the Democratic nominee "needs to focus on getting 270 electoral votes, not 370. That doesn't mean you don't have some spares in your pocket, so you are looking at 300 or whatever, but to go to play Missouri and Arizona is not that sensible a strategy. Focus is very important. There is going to be a lot of interest in places like Texas, for instance, that look like a shiny object at the moment—it may be winnable— but, boy, you better be pretty sure about it before you go spending all the time and money it takes to win in Texas."

"Don't get greedy, don't get stupid," says another strategist. "You want to reshape the party? Win the election, get Trump out of the White House. Then you can strengthen the party."

Often Democrats will see one or two early autumn polls that suggest a close race in a major, long-shot state, fantasize about all the benefits of a win—the enticingly big vote haul, the debilitating psychological warfare—and convince themselves to make a late play. In 2020, there will almost certainly be polls of this nature in some delectable, elusive states, determined by the identity and strengths of the nominee and the running mate who ends up on the Democratic ticket. Given how often the strategists press for an offensive strategy against the incumbent, such a move might seem doubly inviting, since it will force Team Trump to divert its capital and will needle its cutthroat leader.

But the collective guidance of the strategists, who advocate running a daring campaign but urge caution about trying to expand the map, produces the chief riddle of the 2020 election and the ultimate paradox for Democrats hoping to oust Donald Trump. Going for 270 electoral votes with the Clinton states plus the Big 3 is, in one sense, the safest bet, and in another sense extraordinarily risky. Safe bets are only safe when they pay off. "You have to have more than a three-state strategy," says Sebelius. "Starting with no margin of error is a very dangerous thing to do."

While the nation is undergoing demographic changes that would make a candidate with Trump's profile unelectable down the road, he remains a strong candidate in 2020. And the electorate in the Big 3 is whiter and older than the country as a whole. Their populations are aging at a faster rate than the national average and, as age correlates with ideology, they have seen a declining number of self-identified liberals over the last decade. These states arguably are hospitable to Trump's message, at least now through November 3.

· · ·

Trump himself, for all his madcap idiosyncrasies as president, has many of the same advantages enjoyed by fellow modern incumbents Bill Clinton, George W. Bush, and Barack Obama. He has well-funded coffers, no apparent serious challenge for the nomination, the support of a unified party, and a consistent theory of the case. The 270 electoral votes are well within his sights even if he loses the national popular vote.

No one knows how many votes will be required for a candidate to emerge victorious in each battleground state. Most strategists and analysts believe turnout will be higher in 2020 than in 2016, perhaps substantially so, although a significant portion of that additional turnout will come from states such as California and New York, where a large margin of victory—even if larger still than Clinton's—will have no impact on the final outcome. National popular vote wins are meaningless.

So how many votes does the Democratic nominee require to win Wisconsin? Michigan? Pennsylvania? If the experts are correct, and national turnout is higher, the Democrat will almost certainly need more votes in those states than Clinton received, perhaps considerably more.

Although Trump's actions as president have not appeared to broaden his appeal, the strategists note that he nevertheless might draw in new voters. The experts also say that Trump and his allies could depress Democratic turnout by tarnishing the image of the nominee and micro-targeting messages to specific demographics, persuading some voters to stay home from the polls or not vote on the presidential line.

The Michigan strategist Jill Alper has invoked the phrase "begin with the end in mind." Mirroring that concept, let's end with the beginning in mind, and ask Paul Tully's friend Will Robinson how the fabled mastermind, so essential to the last successful challenge to an incumbent, would find the proper number of votes in the proper states to beat Trump.

"Channeling Tully," says Robinson, "it is not just the emerging electorate and it is not just blue-collar, former Trump supporters. It is both. We don't have enough of the rising American electorate to be able to win just on that, and there are still pockets of areas that we need to talk to some of these white voters." In the progressive movement, Robinson continues, "you have that discussion about going after these blue-collar white voters and people get upset because you're not talking about Latinos."

"I think Tully would have a series of slides on the huge rising American electorate vote, youth vote, Latino vote," Robinson says. "I know Paul would be cautioning people about the Latino vote being taken for granted and the African American vote being taken for granted. But then Tully would have a series of slides—Greater Minnesota, southeastern Ohio, southwestern Pennsylvania—that would have Trump vote growth off of Obama vote, and then the partial recovery, to complete recovery of that vote in some areas [in 2018] and identify the areas where we would need to continue that effort.

"A presidential election and an off-year election are two different animals," Robinson clarifies. "You can learn something from the midterms, but they are two different electorates, and we need to look at the presidential electorate. I don't think we can grow our way out of this situation [with more votes from the rising electorate]; I think we also need to persuade [more white voters]."

Robinson adds, "I have dreams about Paul sometimes. I actually had a dream where I was talking this through with Tully."

This advice from beyond the grave matches up with the general strategist opinion about how to find more votes this time around. The focus should be on non-white voters; young voters; suburban voters, especially women; and on cutting into Trump's margin among white, working-class and rural voters. The intent should not be merely rebuilding the winning Obama coalition, but on mounting supplementary support on top of that coalition, with specialized adjustments based on which candidate wins the nomination.

Says Governor Granholm, "Obviously there has been this false binary choice that has been debated inside of the Democratic Party about whether you put your most important effort into getting out the base or whether you put any effort at all into persuasion. I think it is a false choice. I think you have to do both. Democrats in 2020 have to defend every blade of grass. From my perspective in Michigan, the Clinton campaign was sort of a case in point in this because they put a huge amount of effort into getting out the base, but less effort into persuasion of rural and exurban voters.

"Obama won those voters by a larger margin than Hillary Clinton did because he did have such a program, and he is the one who will say, today, you need to persuade those voters," Granholm says. "You cannot leave people behind, especially since they are the ones who are most negatively affected, particularly by tariffs, or feel betrayed because of the plants closing down, when he said he would keep these jobs, or because of the opioid epidemic, which he hasn't fixed, or because their health care has been taken away because Donald Trump has trashed the Affordable Care Act."

One strategist working for a leading 2020 candidate worries that too often there has been an emphasis on reaching white voters, without allocating sufficient means to ensuring that, beyond standard get-out-the-vote rallies held immediately before Election Day, members of the Obama coalition of the ascendant who are registered to vote actually cast ballots. "Not treating African American voters and Latino voters as persuasion targets in 2020 and just as get-out-the-vote targets is a mistake," she says. "I think there has been a long-standing Democratic Party practice of not spending money to communicate with those key, core communities during the persuasion part of the campaign. I like to say that spending $12 million to reach five undecided white voters in some county as opposed to spending it to really go build, support, and motivate people to vote [is a mistake]. There's traditionally been, in my mind, a hole between registration, where people spend a lot of money on registration, and then get out the vote the last two or three weeks where you have these crazy get-out-the-vote rallies, right? But, increasingly, there's a big piece of this where you cannot, and where I think the Democratic Party should not, take for granted that in October they will be able to motivate people to get to the polls. They need to think about spending money to engage with those communities as much as they spend to engage with your white, unemployed, manufacturing person in Wisconsin.

"You can't just push a button and expect people to show up," she continues. "But this is what this party has been doing. Obviously, because Barack Obama was on the ballot, it was a little easier to get people to show up and stand in line for four hours in Chesapeake, Virginia, when there were only two voting booths. But they are not going to stand in line for four hours for everybody unless you've actually been communicating with them the way you would communicate with any other kind of voter you care about."

Pete Giangreco agrees that there are numerous voters out there—persuadables and sympathizers—who have been neglected by the party, a potentially egregious oversight when the stakes are so high. "We still need to compete in rural areas. We cannot get blown out there the way Hillary Clinton did. Part of that was a cultural thing." Also, he says, "We had a lot of people who stayed home, especially in the states where the Clinton campaign did not invest anything on the ground. Wisconsin is a perfect example. One of the many reasons they lost Wisconsin, in addition to never going there, not being on the air there, not spending any money there, is the youth vote was down in places like Madison, and the African American vote was down in places like the north side of Milwaukee. So we left a lot of people on the table because there are a lot of Democrats who either thought Hillary was going to win, just didn't think their vote mattered, and/or they didn't like her and/or they were not energized. And they stayed home. So there is some gold in some states that we have not mined," that will counteract Trump's potentially greater support in rural and working-class areas.

"But," he concludes, "I think in the end, the way we win is, we have got to do better in the suburbs than Hillary did, which is daunting. She did well in the suburbs. But a lot of the 2018 candidates, whether they were gubernatorial candidates or congressional candidates, they ran ahead of her. And that's what we've got to continue to do. And they did it by talking about health care and economic insecurity. Trump is going to talk about the sunshine and we're going to talk about the clouds that are gathering on the horizon. And we'll see who wins."

"It's simple arithmetic," says Donna Brazile. If Trump "is able to regain his footing with suburban white women and there is no effort to bring black and Latino turnout to what we saw in 2012, we lose."

There is no avoiding this truth. The Democratic nominee must find new voters, or fall short. Team Trump has spent the last three years on a voter quest of its own. There are liberals living within their anti-Trump bubbles who cannot fathom that citizens all across the country who did not vote for Trump in 2016, will do so in 2020. "It seems hard for many people to believe," says one strategist. "They look at Trump with his manic outbursts and his contempt for the Constitution. The babies ripped from their parents at the border and stuck in filthy detention centers, no one changing their diapers or rocking them to sleep. All of Trump's crazy tweets and policy pronouncements that go nowhere. The obvious racism. The gun violence that seems committed in his honor. He's a joke all over Europe and Asia. Who would vote for this man, now that we see what he's capable of? Well, they're out there. The guy has been president almost a full term, and the world is still standing. They've got some more money in their pockets, maybe. He puts America first. They are out there."

They are out there, and Republicans are counting on it. Pete Giangreco believes new Trump voters might exist in large numbers. "He has an appeal for people who did not even vote for him in 2016. Who sort of like all this divisive, negative branding. I think there is still a sleeper cell of people who culturally want to go back to the 1950s, who didn't vote in 2016. They live all over the place. Not so much in cities. But they live in the suburbs, they live in the exurbs, they live particularly in rural areas. There are a lot of thirty-year-old, non-college white women, who probably are not making much money, they are waiting tables, they are working two or three jobs, their kids are not going to stay in small-town America. They have got to go someplace. And they may not have voted last time. And they are going to vote for this guy because he culturally is planting the flag and saying, 'Things were better back when. I want to go back to that.'" Most significantly, says Giangreco, "I think Trump can run up the score in rural areas even bigger than he did."

The strategists also are conscious that 2020 is expected to be an excruciatingly close election. In individual battleground states, unique little clusters of voters could be decisive. Such tiny knots of the electorate are difficult to pinpoint and persuade, but Team Trump has had years to locate and target them. Says Craig Smith, "One-percent elections are field elections. Somebody wins by ten, they won on message. Somebody who wins by one, they won on field. We have to run aggressive and smart field campaigns, and we've got to micro target these groups in the states." As in Florida, Smith says, "Trump is targeting the Venezuelan community by saying 'I'm tough on [anti-American president Nicolás] Maduro, and I'm going to stand up to him.' Now, look, how many votes are there in that community in Florida? A hundred thousand? Hillary lost by 110,000. So you have got to be very smart. The Trump people are very smart in what they are doing. We need to be smart, too."

Part of being smart, Kathleen Sebelius says, is taking support and guidance from the Democratic elected officials in battleground states who have recently won statewide races. People like Michigan governor Gretchen Whitmer, who was elected in 2018 with 53 percent of the vote; Pennsylvania governor Tom Wolf, who won reelection in 2018 with nearly 58 percent; Pennsylvania senator Bob Casey, who won his own reelection with 56 percent; and Wisconsin's Democratic senator, Tammy Baldwin, who won reelection in 2018 with 55 percent of the vote (which, in deeply divided Wisconsin, is a major landslide), along with the state's new governor, Tony Evers, who won narrowly.

These winners, Sebelius explains, are "models of how you do this and how you turn out the vote, not looking back to [the 2016 presidential race], but at the last, most successful Democrats" in each state "and say, 'What did they do, and how did they do it, and how can they be involved, and how can they turn out that vote?' This is going to be an all-hands-on-deck effort. Involvement by these governors and senators who know their states inside and out and how to run a ground campaign based on what we know works is the best way to go after it."

In recent years, campaigns in both parties, along with companies and organizations across the globe, have been transitioning gradually from old-school thirty-second television commercials to sophisticated digital spending. This is an area in which the Trump campaign will almost certainly have a major advantage. Such a concept may seem incongruous given the president's archaic, meat-and-potatoes, men-are-from-Mars, Luddite persona, but Trump's campaign manager, Brad Parscale, is a digital savant and new media expert, and the 2020 campaign's earliest spending has been focused on amplifying the success Team Trump had in this field four years ago, especially on Facebook.

The strategists assume that outside groups, including foreign entities supportive of Trump's effort, will also be highly active on the digital landscape in finding, targeting, and turning out voters, as well as in voter suppression, often working below the radar, if not with total invisibility. Such clandestine exercises, executed in the closing weeks of the campaign, will be difficult to identify and expose, and targeted voters will have few ways to determine who is behind the messages, what is true, and what is not.

Again, the strategists call attention to just how close a race this is likely to be, and observe that Trump's head start in the digital arena could be what decides the election in his favor. The Democratic nominee will be able to receive aid from friendly allies who can perform these digital operations, but if by fall the campaign has not devoted a sizable percentage of its resources to all dimensions of the digital world, it will not have a chance in November.

"It's really all about social media," Robinson says. "Seventy percent of the world is on Facebook, the younger kids are on Insta. How do you reach a forty-year-old single mom? She doesn't have time to go to a meeting; you have to reach her at eleven at night while she's waiting for the laundry to come out of the dryer, and that's where we can have that conversation."

Of course, plenty of voters, particularly older citizens who actually vote, dutifully and diligently, still get their campaign pushes, prods, and propaganda from cozy, old-fashioned devices and delivery systems. Basic cable television, one-minute radio ads, newspaper flyers, direct mail. The Trump campaign is well aware that there are retro platforms, including some that shriek *anachronism*, that must also be utilized. The challenge of finding the right mix of old and new media is complex, and once again, Team Trump's long-range planning gives his side a major competitive boost.

Such a comprehensive, varied undertaking requires intricate planning and good sense. Says Granholm, "I don't think you can do this just by taking out generic ads on CNN or NBC. You have to go to where these voters get their news. So, for example, in rural Michigan, most people don't have Sirius XM in their car. They're listening to AM radio for news, weather, and sports. And so if you're going to reach them, you have to reach them where they get their news, whether it's on Facebook in a very targeted way or local news, which is still trusted."

   •   •   •

Paul Tully's main device for solving the Electoral College Rubik's Cube was a spreadsheet that ranked the states in descending order from the likelihood they would vote for the Democrat to the likelihood they would vote Republican.

Here is what a version of the Tully chart would look like for 2020:

State	Electoral Votes	Clinton 2016	Dem Top of Ticket 2018	Dem Running Total	GOP Running Total	State	Electoral Votes	Trump 2016	GOP Top of Ticket 2018	Running Total
Bankable States										
DC	3	90.9%	79.5%	3						3
HI	4	62.2%	62.7%	7						7
CA	55	61.7%	61.3%	62						62
MA	11	60.0%	60.3%	73						73
MD	10	60.3%	64.2%	83						83
VT	3	56.7%	67.4%	86						86
NY	29	59.0%	59.0%	115						115
IL	20	55.8%	54.2%	135						135
WA	12	52.5%	58.7%	147						147
RI	4	54.4%	52.8%	151						151
NJ	14	55.5%	53.7%	165						165
CT	7	54.6%	49.2%	172						172
DE	3	53.4%	60.0%	175						175
OR	7	50.1%	50.0%	182						182
Lean Democratic										
NM	5	48.3%	57.1%	187						187
VA	13	49.8%	56.9%	200						200
CO	9	48.2%	52.3%	209						209
NV	6	47.9%	49.4%	215						215
Battleground (Tier 1)										
MN	10	46.4%	53.9%	225	323					225
MI	16	47.3%	53.3%	241	313					241
PA	20	47.9%	57.7%	261	297					261
WI	10	46.5%	49.6%	271	277					271
Battleground (Tier 2)										
ME	3	47.8%	50.8%	274	267					274
NH	4	46.8%	45.8%	278	264					278
FL	29	47.8%	49.2%	307	260					307
Battleground (Tier 3)										
ME	1	44.9%	43.2%	308	231					308
AZ	11	48.1%	48.0%	319	230					319
NC	15	49.8%	N/A	334	219					334
OH	18	51.7%	46.8%	352	204					352
IA	6	51.1%	50.4%	358	186					358
GA	16	50.8%	50.3%	374	180					374
Lean Republican										
					164	TX	38	52.2%	50.9%	412
Solid Republican										
					126	MT	3	56.2%	47.0%	415
					123	SC	9	54.9%	54.0%	424
					114	AK	3	51.3%	52.3%	427
					111	UT	6	45.5%	62.9%	433
					105	MS	6	57.9%	58.0%	439
					99	MO	10	56.8%	51.5%	449
					89	IN	11	56.9%	51.0%	460
					78	LA	8	58.1%	N/A	468
					70	KS	6	56.7%	43.3%	474
					64	NE	5	58.7%	59.4%	479
					59	TN	11	60.7%	54.7%	490
					48	AR	6	60.6%	65.4%	496
					42	AL	9	62.1%	59.6%	505
					33	SD	3	61.5%	51.0%	508
					30	KY	8	62.5%	N/A	516
					22	ID	4	59.2%	60.0%	520
					18	ND	3	63.0%	55.5%	523
					15	OK	7	65.3%	54.3%	530
					8	WV	5	68.6%	46.3%	535
					3	WY	3	68.2%	67.1%	538

Tully lived in a world overflowing with data, but in 1992, he distilled the information into a simple numerical formula that cracked the code, isolated the votes, and secured the Electoral College for Bill Clinton of Arkansas. Tully stored his figures in his brain, wore his heart on his sleeve, and kept his confidence stoked. His compatriot Ron Brown, who died in a plane crash in 1996 in Croatia while serving as Clinton's Secretary of Commerce, was perhaps more polished and more sedate, but his optimism brimmed with equal force.

This chart displays just how central the Big 3 states, Pennsylvania, Michigan, and Wisconsin, will be in determining the 2020 outcome and just how small the number of states and voters deciding the election will be if it is close.

In a tight race, of course, any action, by candidate, campaign, or outside force, can precipitate a defeat. As the country begins its relentless march to the voting booth, it is notable just how many Democratic strategists are anticipating a Trump reelection. They cannot divine how the challenger will have a proper plan in place to manage the myriad twists and turns of 2020, the underhanded schemes and ruthless adversaries, especially at the end of the race when there will be less time to recover from a stumble or a splat.

And, too often, they have seen Democratic candidates felled by inaction, diffidence, misplaced principle, naiveté. "You can't run not to lose," admonishes Kathleen Sebelius. "I have watched too many candidates do that over and over again. Too cautious, too this, too that. At the end of the day, voters immediately sense that the person is not authentic. So that's a big mistake."

It is essential, a number of strategists insist, for the Democrat to vault into the race against Trump with absolute certainty that the president is too unpopular to win a second term. One strategist, famous for his own meticulous planning and unwavering confidence throughout the ups and downs of two winning presidential campaigns, says that members of the Democratic Party "were blown away by the fact that Trump won last time around, and they have not gotten their heads around why he has stayed alive this long. This guy has survived things that would have blown up a previous White House and decimated a previous president. But, yet, he just sort of gets up in the morning and starts tweeting away, and by God they don't know what to do about it. I think this thing is going to depend upon how so many things play out on each and every day," he says. "Now, can he win? Yes."

Not so fast. Many experts—equally seasoned, equally savvy, equally scrupulous—see a far graver direction for the president. Karl Rove, the longtime George W. Bush advisor, continues, "Can he lose? Yes. Is this thing as bad as the Democrats think? No."

Rove acknowledges that Trump won in 2016 at least in part because a lot of voters did not want to support Hillary Clinton. A more palatable 2020 Democratic candidate produces a difficult math challenge for Trump, both nationally and, more importantly, in the battleground states. "The danger that Trump faces in 2020," Rove says, "is that he has a very energized, hard-core base, but that hard-core base is in the low forties and the question is, how do you get, not just to the forty-six that he got last time around, but a higher percentage than that?"

Rove supports Trump's reelection. Despite that, he has a more jaundiced view of the incumbent's prospects than almost any Democrat interviewed for this book. In fact, that is true of all the other Republicans who were consulted, some of whom back the president, and some of whom are openly anti-Trump. This pattern suggests that the Democratic analysis might be shaded by the sheer terror brought on by the prospect of four more years of Donald J. Trump, President.

Mike Murphy, who advised Bob Dole, John McCain, Mitt Romney, and several other presidential hopefuls, says, "The

Democrats are all mind fucked by Trump. It is amazing. It's like Rasputin. They just think he can't be killed because a whole bunch of other people, including me, said he was going to lose the last election. And he won. So therefore, 'He's got magic and can't be beat.' That's all bullshit."

As many other Republican and Democratic strategists contend, Murphy says the most dangerous move the Democrats can make is to nominate someone too liberal to be an acceptable choice. "I think voters are tired of Trump, and I think he is going to lose," says Murphy. "The only chance he has is the Democrats give him something to work with."

Unlike Rove, Murphy will not vote for Trump. But he will not cast a ballot for the Democratic option either, and intends to write in the name of a Republican politician whom he admires. But he is nearly certain the Democrats will triumph next November 3, especially if the nominee exploits Trump's inherent weaknesses and the disdain he has roused in the electorate these past few years.

"Trump is the easiest candidate to predict strategically, not always tactically, of anybody," says Murphy. "So you know what the strategy is going to be—'welfare bums, left-wing socialism.' He's one-note. It's a powerful note, but it's one note, and he's played it. He's got the biggest microphone in politics, the presidency, but fundamentally voters want to fire him, so work with that. I don't think you have to vilify Trump—that is built in. You just have to roll your eyes at him." Murphy suggests baiting Trump as an easy mark. "Have a very good surrogate team that he will not ignore," he says. "Move in on Fox News. If you want to get in his head, get on Fox."

"Remember," Murphy adds, "he is the most insecure guy in the world and you can get into his head. So have a team of psychologists to help you work that through in your rhetoric. Don't ape him but contrast with him with strength. That's the key. You can't look weak with Trump. Keep the offense on him, which is middle-class economics and his raw incompetence. 'Trump the chump. He's been rolled by the North Koreans. He's Putin's ventriloquist dummy. He doesn't know how to be president. He's a silly, insecure guy. His nickname is "Needy Donald."'"

Murphy thinks George W. Bush and Barack Obama were able to overcome adversity and get reelected because they exhibited a flexibility and nimbleness that the current occupant of the Oval Office lacks. "Trump is incredibly different from any other candidate that we have ever had," he says. "When you are a president in trouble, like Bush was at the time, like Obama was, if you are smart, you can change, and you can use the apparatus of the White House to reorient. You can run a strategic campaign because you can have a strategy. Trump has none of those things. He's the atomic clock of Trump. He has one reaction, every situation, which is what you would hear at a kitchen table in Queens, 1963. So he's a one-hit wonder. He has shown no ability to change or adapt to his strategic advantage. He just keeps going back to play the Republican primary game. So unlike Bush and unlike Obama, I don't think he can heal himself."

"But," says Murphy, tossing in the caveat, "if the Democrats nominate a candidate who falls neatly into the only strategy Trump has, which is race and cultural division, then he can beat them."

Bill Kristol, the longtime Republican tactician who worked in the George H.W. Bush White House, is even further along the anti-Trump spectrum, openly preferring most of the Democratic candidates to the incumbent. And he is even more optimistic that Trump will be beaten, although he acknowledges that the challenging party is haunted by history.

"Everyone is spooked because they thought they were going to beat the last three incumbents, and they didn't, but you can overlearn that lesson," he says. "I still come back to the core:

Trump's reasonably low level of approval, especially given the economy. Replicate the 2018 elections as much as possible," which, he argues, were a referendum on Trump. Do that and he is done and dusted. "There's an awful lot of unhappiness with his conduct as president. As long as the alternative is respectable. The one thing that people haven't focused on," says Kristol, is "what a Trump second term would look like. We will make it through four years of Trump, but isn't eight years awfully risky?"

Risky. It is a word the Democratic strategists often use, to describe the angles and approaches, the plots and tactics a campaign might apply to navigate the choppy, perilous waters of a high-stakes race. But for many, the looming 2020 battle against Donald Trump is about far more than risk. It is about more than enduring a nail-biting finale as the votes roll in, election night theme songs swelling on the network broadcasts, and social media buzzing with the hashtag #2020ishere. It is about more than tolerating a stinging election loss, reattaching scuffed "Not My President" bumper stickers, tuning in again to partisan TV, and grumbling about impeachment. For them, it is about preventing a great American disaster, a great American tragedy, a deep, irreparable wound to the soul of the country.

America has already changed fundamentally because of the presidency of Donald Trump. The United States is still a very young country, just a few hundred years old. Greece has five thousand years on us. England has more than a thousand. Other presidencies have altered our character. Lincoln made us stronger. FDR made us braver. The assassination of JFK made us more mature. The resignation of Nixon made us more sober. The impeachment of Clinton made us more jaded. But the election of Trump has knocked us permanently off balance, as citizens and as a nation. A reality TV show host, with little apparent understanding of policy, governance, or decorum, has taken us all on a wild ride where facts have become agents of evil, foreign dictators have become role models, and innocent children have become criminals, locked up and devalued.

No longer are Democrats, their friends, and colleagues, their acquaintances abroad, asking the question that echoed again and again after election night 2016: *How could this have happened?* Nor are they asserting, *Well, it won't happen again, not after this.* Now they are simply afraid. Afraid of four more years and what it will mean.

They can hope that the Democratic candidate who is selected to challenge the president will have a plan to beat him. And they can hope that the nominee will have the confidence required to get it done.

Defeating an incumbent president is exceedingly difficult. To approach such a task with confidence might be considered irrational, foolhardy, futile. Yet Ron Brown and Paul Tully found that confidence in 1992. Yes, they had a strong plan for raising money, counting votes, uniting the party. But they surveyed the conditions of America, its heart, its soul, its economy, its people, and they recognized that, as formidable as George H. W. Bush seemed to be, they had a better story to tell in 1992. They told the story of an economy that was not serving its working people. They told a story of a man from Hope. They found a candidate who could talk the owls down from the trees. They found the story America needed to hear.

How do you beat Trump? With a candidate who knows that the story she or he can tell is better than the story the incumbent can tell. It won't be a story that merely sounds better than Hillary Clinton's anemic tale. It will be a story that appeals to Democrats and Republicans and independents, to the people who stayed home in 2016, or voted for the Green Party, or, yes, who voted for Trump.

A Democratic nominee with a strong, true American story will have the confidence to beat this president, and that story, that confidence, can inspire a movement. Listen closely. If all goes well for the Democrats, if the candidates heed all this advice and the nominee stays strong, the rallying cry will not be "*Trump can be beaten*," but "*Trump will be beaten*."

ACKNOWLEDGMENTS

To Judith Regan: I am grateful for your encouragement and inspiration, awed by your accomplishments and strength, and honored to get to work with a publishing legend who is at the top of her game.

Thanks to Mitchell Jackson and the rest of the Regan Arts team for cleverness and professionalism beyond compare.

Adam P. Fox was tireless, brilliant, and cheerful in assisting with all aspects of the book. His future is as bright as he is.

This book would not exist without the generous cooperation of the political strategists who spent hours patiently walking me through their plans and hopes (and fears) about Donald Trump and 2020. Thank you one and all for sharing.

I am thankful to my family, friends, neighbors, and colleagues for their support and love in my three favorite time periods—past, present, and future.

Mark Halperin